U-237 IN THE DEVIL'S TRIANGLE

THE U-237 IN THE DEVIL'S TRIANGLE

BY

JOHN M. JONES III

A NEPTUNE BOOK

(FIRST EDITION)

ISBN # 0-914042-03-3
Library of Congress # 75-4195

COVER DESIGN BY SCOTT GUYNUP

This book relates to events which have occurred in the Devil's Triangle but is classified as fiction. Any similarity to persons living or dead is purely coincidental.

NEPTUNE BOOKS is a division of CORAL REEF PUBLICATIONS, INC., 45 6th Street SW, Winter Haven, Fl 33880

DEDICATION

To my wife Mary Lou who insisted I keep writing.

ACKNOWLEDGEMENTS

My thanks to Carolyn Mickler who helped me place these thoughts into words.

PREFACE

This story, partially based on facts pertaining to certain dates when disappearances did occur in the Devil's Triangle, offers the reader a possible solution as to the cause of such phenomena.

But what is more consequential is the fictional parallel of conditions on the planet SPECTRA in relation to those now on EARTH.

The Editors

TABLE OF CONTENTS

FOREWORD

The Devil's Triangle refers to an area in the Atlantic Ocean that has a reputation for causing ships, planes and people to disappear without a trace. What happens? Why is nothing ever found? This book will attempt to explain the effects of an underground pyramid which is causing compasses and navigational devices to become useless, and why great fear is experienced by those entering into the Devil's Triangle . . . for it is said this region is avoided with good reason by seamen.

By combining findings from several exploration reports with my own research, it was possible to provide the background for this book. For it is a fact that there are huge ancient stones and twenty story buildings submerged in this area . . . not to mention old pirate's wells being discovered on the islands in this area off the Florida coast.

I discussed my findings from explorations in this area — on a daily basis for a period of three months — with a man of German descent who was obsessed with the idea of discovering GOLD. Armed with my information, he would study old charts and maps, plot courses and draw new charts. He made detailed investigations of the last known location of downed planes and sunken ships and plotted the exact spots where he expected to find their remains.

His last dive occurred in 1965. One evening, around midnight, he had just completed charting his course and knew his destination. As soon as he finished his calculations he immediately drove to Key West and made final preparations for his dive at dawn of the following day.

The dive produced the remains of an old ship, but no GOLD. He returned home seriously ill from ulcers which eventually caused his death a few weeks later. During his last week alive, he asked his wife to call me and relay this message. "CHECK 28° N – 77.5° W, YET 200 MILES OFF IN A TRIANGLE."

I knew his gift of this information could be one of wealth, perhaps GOLD, but I realized his obsession with this search had, to a great extent, proved fatal – which is a consequence I wish to avoid.

Therefore, as of March 15, 1974, after compiling this information and presented here, I say to all who read the following – imagine, comprehend, concentrate and you will possibly find more than GOLD.

John M. Jones III

CHAPTER I

The German submarine U-237, at 2000 hours on the evening of April 13, 1945, had just surfaced for air somewhere in the Atlantic near the Azores. The night was still, the stars bright against a dark heaven — offering a quiet interlude in a noisy war-torn and conflict-ravaged world. The gently rolling waves belied the storm-tortured waters of a few hours ago, now calm after an early storm of near hurricane force. The crewmen, accustomed to such quirks of nature, after three years of working together as a team, seldom talked about the storms. More often they talked about their homes and families, dreams of what they would do when the war was over, and girls they had known or hoped to know in the future.

As the hatches began to open, forty-two of the fifty-four man crew emerged on deck, each one filling his lungs full of fresh sea air. How good the slight burning sensation felt to their throats; how clean the atmosphere was after the storm. It was marvelous being able to lie on deck and relax; to look at the sky and enjoy the serenity.

On the conning tower, Captain Willis Brunt stretched to his full six-foot height. His lean body began to feel refreshed as the stale air was exhaled and some of the weariness left him. Years of seafaring had turned his face to the color and texture of newly-tanned leather; years of war had etched deep lines into a perpetual expression of concern and distress. Now at thirty-six, Captain Brunt wondered if he had ever been young. It seemed he had always been in the middle of strife and battle.

Beside the Captain stood another man looking too old for his years. A doctor at twenty-eight, he appeared physically very tired, although mentally very alert. Only the deep blue eyes gave his despair away, for outwardly Doctor Eric von Wilhelm was a fine example of the Arian German youth. His closely cut blond hair and handsome face gave him the smart appearance expected of young German officers. He proudly bore a sabre nick on his left cheek, the only blemish on his clean-shaven face.

Captain Brunt requested their position from the navigator, Carl Hinze, a well-educated twenty year old German who had already completed his college courses and was studying advanced curriculum subjects.

Carl relayed their position in the Atlantic to the Captain. "Heading 0° — Position 30° West, 38° North, Sir."

"Thank you," replied Captain Brunt. Then turning to Doctor von Wilhelm, and with pain and sadness in his eyes, asked of Eric, "What is to come of all this? I begin to wonder. Germany is surely lost. You and I know this is a hard fact to accept, but true nevertheless. What will the future hold for us? For our men? For our country? I know you were in the Nazi Youth Movement, one of Hitler's children. Maybe you can give me a decent answer?"

Eric von Wilhelm maintained his stare at the distant stars. Without turning he replied, "I have given the matter much thought. I agree that having been raised by Hitler should give me some greater insight, some inkling of what may happen next . . . but I have no answer. Only questions come to mind. Did you know that I was forced to study all the time? Not only my medical training, but history of all ages, languages, ancient writings, even one full year of advanced engineering? Then, I was forced . . . now, I thirst to know the stars, the planets, and the universe; to discover their secrets and their power over men."

Eric suddenly realized he hadn't fully answered the Captain. "What is the answer? What next? All that comes to mind are deep philosophical questions which surely won't help us right now. I would need to know what our situation is right now. How much food we have. How much fuel. What possible alternative action do we have. What are the practical aspects of the present situation. Perhaps by assessing these we can chart a course for our future."

After careful consideration, Captain Brunt responded. "We have a full store of food; fuel, if it were stretched, could last about six weeks — a range of 1200 miles. Do you contemplate surrender?"

"NEVER!" replied von Wilhelm angrily. "WE WILL NOT SURRENDER! We will make a break . . . start a new life . . . begin all over again."

"What do you mean, a new life?"

"We will find an unknown island. Somewhere in this vast ocean there must be an undiscovered parcel of land we can inhabit. Perhaps we should begin the search now," said Eric thoughtfully.

"But what about the crew, Eric? They should be a part of this decision, too. They have a right to choose," asserted the Captain.

"You're right, of course. We will discuss the possibilities and alternatives with them and take a vote. We will act as individuals from now on, as free men able to determine actions on our own and not subject to direct orders from a chain of command hierarchy. Free to choose our destiny!"

"Captain! Captain!" shouted Hinze. "Planes sighted at 10 o'clock and closing fast, sir!"

"Time enough later to think about the future; at present we must survive. DIVE! DIVE!! Sound the alarm! DIVE!" commanded the Captain.

Moments later, Ensign Melvin Schmidt, the Sonar/Radar Operator reported the planes directly overhead.

"Brace for bombs!" ordered Captain Brunt. "Brace!"

Then came a succession of four quick blasts. As the sub shuddered from the blasts, it maintained its dive.

"What is our depth?" shouted Brunt.

"Sixty feet and diving sir," replied Schmidt.

"Thank God! We're out of danger now."

"Level at 100 feet, sir," Schmidt informed the Captain.

"Maintain 20 knots," directed the Captain tersely. Then stillness. All was quiet until the silence was broken by Schmidt.

"Sub chasers! Closing in fast!"

"Prepare for depth charges . . . take her down . . . go to 300 feet," ordered Brunt.

Then it began. Far away at first, then coming closer. One, then another . . . a little louder . . . a little closer. Explosions resounded within the sub. It was almost like a countdown. Crewmen all deathly-still waiting for the one big blast. Everything seemed to have stopped.

Suddenly the waiting was over. Contact! The sub had been hit. Lights flickered, dimmed, flickered again and died. The ship rolled, rocked and churned. Leaks sprang everywhere as the shock waves began reverberating.

"Switch to auxiliary power," commanded Brunt. Everything was shaking; and as the sub began to slowly stabilize, the rolling grew slower; the rocking subsided. "All stations report immediately."

"Torpedo Room . . . one man injured here, sir. Can the doctor come?" Eric quickly responded and went forward.

"Chaser returning!" warned Schmidt. "Moving in fast!"

"Brace!" commanded the Captain.

Once more the waiting began. The explosions getting nearer and nearer. Finally the blast and ear-splitting whine as they were hit again. Water poured in everywhere.

Within minutes the depth charges stopped and finally Schmidt cried out, "The chasers are leaving! Appear to be heading South, sir!"

"We will sit calm," instructed Brunt, as a deep sigh escaped his lips.

Profound relief swept through the crew. It had been a brutal attack — nearly disabling. Captain Brunt requested additional damage reports from all stations as he wiped a small trickle of blood from his forehead.

"Bridge here sir, reporting all sections secure. Forward torpedo room still flooding though."

"We are on the bottom, sir," reported Navigator Hinze, as other section leaders reported in with their assessments of damage sustained. It appeared from first reports that only structural damage had been inflicted by the depth charges.

"Leaks now sealed in forward torpedo room, sir. One man – Richter – is dead."

Heads lowered as the Captain requested further reports on injured men. Once compiled, Brunt called for all men to comfort the wounded and began his rounds of the ship to check on and assess the damage inflicted to his submarine. It was a depressing tour; many men hurt and dead. The actual damage appeared to be minimal, surprisingly enough; mainly superficial and temporary repairs could be made easily. He picked several crewmen to begin repairs while the others tended to the wounded and dead.

The crew was despondent, for of the original fifty-four men, only twenty-one were now able seamen. Many had sustained fatal head injuries from the severe turmoil and violent rocking of their ship. Eric had not rested in over twenty-four hours, and although extremely efficient, most of the wounded he could not save; his best medical efforts were directed at easing pain and giving comfort.

Captain Brunt ordered all hands to get four hours sleep before resuming duties, for as bone tired as they all were now, very little could be accomplished without some sleep. Only a skeleton crew remained awake for watch duty and basic operations.

Captain Brunt retired to his stateroom but could not rest. "What now?" he thought aloud. "Twenty-one able men in a seventy foot sub, resting on the bottom of an ocean, running on emergency lighting and power, and the oxygen supply dangerously low. What chance do we have now? When we are able to surface, will be the time I gather the men together and propose a vote on our next course of action. Right now though, other matters must be attended to."

Finally he dozed off only to be awakened shortly by his alarm.

The wake-up signal was heard over the intercom notifying the crew that it was time to get about the day's tasks. Captain Brunt appeared in the operations room, "Are the men up and about?"

"Yes, sir everyone is eating breakfast now." Hinze replied.

"It will have to be a quick meal. I want the entire crew ready for action in 15 minutes. And tell them I will talk to them on deck at 0515 sharp."

"Yes sir, I'll make sure they are ready," replied Hinze.

"Sonar. What do you hear now?"

"All clear. All quiet, Captain."

"Very well then, prepare to take her up. Bring her to 30 feet."

The ship began to groan and creak as the heavy nose slowly began to rise, gradually gaining speed. The craft proceeded upward to 30 feet.

"Thirty feet, sir."

"Up periscope. Sonar, give me a current report," ordered Brunt as he scanned the darkness for any shapes or forms on the horizon.

"All clear, sir," replied Schmidt as he completed a 360° scan.

"Good. Surface to conning tower depth. Have Seaman Hiney go out on top and give me a visual sighting."

As Hiney unscrewed the hatch, the Captain, in his mind, began preparing for his discussion with the crew. After learning that Hiney observed the scene on the surface to be clear in all directions, he ordered the submarine to surface.

All available hands fell out on deck gulping in the early morning air as soon as the sub had leveled off, sincerely grateful to be alive and on the surface again.

The dawn's silence seemed to be a prayer of thanksgiving. All was still as Brunt ran his hands over his thinning hair. "Secure from damage. Open all hatches. Have the men prepare to bury our dead with full honors. Seaman Hiney, report to my stateroom at once."

Back below deck, Brunt went to his quarters, sat down heavily in his comfortable leather chair, and buried his head in his folded arms.

A moment later, Hiney knocked at the stateroom. Oscar Hiney was the one crew member that the Captain could count on to brace up his spirits, for although forty was fairly old for a submariner, Brunt was glad to have Hiney aboard. His common sense more than compensated for his lack of formal education, and his wit had made this arduous war a little more bearable.

"Yes, sir? Can I bring the Captain something? I know where a bottle of fine Schnapps is, still intact. Can I bring the Captain some coffee laced with it, sir?"

"Oscar, you are truly worth your weight in gold. Yes, that sounds good. Please bring me a full pot from your 'secret supply' . . . and report back also with an estimate of your galley condition and the supplies that can be utilized. I'll need to know how long you think our stores will last. And would you please ask Ensign Rehrberg to report to me also? Thank you. I'll be available for your report whenever you are ready."

"Okay, sir, I shouldn't be too long."

Oscar quickly found Carl Rehrberg. His light red hair and heavy beard easily distinguished him from the other crew members. Rehrberg, at 5'10" and 210 pounds, was one of the few heavy-set men on board; and also one of the strongest. He could bend a 60 penny nail with his bare hands! Upon hearing that the Captain wished to see him, he made haste to the Captain's quarters and reported that all was in good shape in the engine room.

"What about fuel?" asked the Captain.

"We have enough to run about 1200 miles; by using our batteries, maybe 2000," was Rehrberg's reply.

"Very well. You may secure."

Carl passed Oscar on the way out, already returning with his report and the Captain's coffee.

"I estimate we have supplies for about thirty-five days sir."

"Thank you Hiney . . . and also for this delicious coffee."

Eric finally appeared in the Captain's quarters and began to bandage the wound on the Captain's head while they discussed the recent incident.

"You realize we almost went out that time, Willie."

"Yes, I know, Eric. How about the funeral arrangements for the dead?"

"We are ready to bury them. They were good men. We will surely miss them."

"Eric. Are you ready to ask the men for a vote? I believe all the men will follow our lead now."

"Yes. It seems to me that after the funeral, while all the men are on top, would be the best time to take the vote." With a distant look in his blue eyes, Eric wondered just what indeed would happen to them. Was there any way to foresee the future? His day-dreaming was interrupted by the blare of "ALL HANDS ON DECK!" from the speaker.

All remaining crewmen assembled topside and stood at attention as the time came to pay their respects to their friends and comrades who had been demanded by the sea.

Captain Brunt began, "He that is not prepared to die at all times, is not prepared to live. I now commend your bodies to the depths of the sea — and your souls to God for judgement. Amen."

As the bodies were slipped over the side, all stood quiet, many with tears in their eyes. Then, without turning to face his men, Captain Brunt started to address them. "I have checked all of your files. I find that all but two of you come from Eastern Germany. As you know, the Russians have captured those towns. On the other side, the Americans are advancing on Berlin. Germany is doomed as a nation and we are doomed as seamen unless we surrender. I do not believe I can live as a captive of any country or any person. While we were on the bottom, all I dreamed of was being on the top and free. Now we are on top, but truly, not free. From my point of view, it is as individuals that we must decide our fate. Knowing that your thoughts go first to your families and your homes, wondering what lies there now, I am proposing a vote."

"What do you mean? What is there to vote on? What do you see as our options?" questioned a man from the rear, in a choked voice.

"I mean we should sail out of this bedlam. Leave this war behind us with its destruction and horror. Set sail for parts unknown and trust our ship to the sea. Our only other alternative, as I see it, is to stand fast and fight to the last man in honor of Germany."

Here, Eric spoke up, addressing the men, "I have known for some time that the war is truly lost for Germany. Oscar Hiney and I are the two crew members not from East Germany but I vote with Captain Brunt. I have no desire to lose any more men; no heart to continue the fight. If others of you have different views we will consider them. Any other suggestions are welcome. If any seaman casts a dissenting vote, and wishes to continue fighting in this war, we will do so and I will tend to all of you to the best of my ability. But we must decide now on our course of action."

A very subdued sigh emerged from most crewmen at the same time. All seemed to be thinking very hard on the alternatives presented to them. No one offered suggestions; no one volunteered any new comments. They just stood on deck with concentrated expressions, considering, remembering, wondering. A faraway look passed through many eyes, then returned to face the unknown! What could the sea hold in store for them? What unforeseen events? Difficulties? Mysteries? What indeed lay ahead for them? Would it be better to stay within the realm of the known; stay and fight for the Homeland? Die for a lost country?

Die from unknowns? Or live and discover an entirely new world? Live and find a new life. How could a man decide? What should he consider in evaluating the choices? Was there hope for victory? Most assuredly not. Anyway, can I reconcile being a prisoner? Any clues as to base what the future might hold for them?

Eric broke the silence and intruded into their thoughts. "At some future date, we may be able to return home to Germany. But not now. Now is the time to come to a conclusion regarding our immediate future. One dissenting vote and we stay and fight. Fight for Germany till death overtakes us — one and all. If none, we sail away leaving the war behind us. Now is the time to decide. All of you could think for days, and still be no closer to a decision than you are now. But there are no days available to stretch our consideration. Ponder only a few minutes more and decide. If you vote to strike out for parts unknown, proceed to the lower deck. If anyone remains on top, we stay at war and fight for Germany."

Captain Brunt was the first one down, followed by Eric. Then slowly a line formed, and single file, the men descended. Carl Rehrberg brought up the rear and announced to the Captain, "No hands remaining on deck, sir. We are our own Navy."

"Secure to dive!" ordered Brunt. "Come to heading 240°, Speed — 15 knots. Sonar, we wish to avoid all ships. Torpedo room . . . prepare to unload all heavy fighting equipment including torpedoes. When ready, fire at will," commanded Captain Brunt.

"Sir," Schmidt spoke up, "shouldn't we keep the torpedoes? We may need them to defend ourselves."

"No son, we will fight no more," said the Captain. "And we must lighten our load to conserve fuel."

"Torpedo room reporting, sir. All orders carried out as directed."

"Very well, thank you. Gentlemen, all hands, this is the Captain speaking. I say to you gladly that we are all free men now. However, until our status changes, that is with the end of this war, we will run submerged during daylight hours, and on top at night. The first chance we get we will paint over all numbers and markings and ready our ship for living."

Eric marked the time, "0730 hours, April 17, 1945. Bearing 240° – Speed – 15 knots. Truly a time, day and place to remember."

CHAPTER II

"What is our present bearing, Ensign Hinze?" inquired Captain Brunt after two days at sea.

"Presently 40° West, 33° North," was Hinze's reply.

"Come to Bearing 250 for the next 20 hours, at 15 knots." The time of day was 2100 hours, April 19th. All crew members were busy painting, cleaning, and rearranging their quarters. Oscar, the cook, had become a truly creative genius in the preparation of the meals. Even though stores were low and the meals originating from cans, delicious smells continued to come from the galley where tasty concoctions appeared nightly for dinner.

The next day at 1700 hours, Eric asked the Captain, "Should we change course now, or continue on as set?"

"What is our present position?"

"45° West 32° North – Bearing 250. Can I ask where we're heading, Willie."

"My best thoughts are to head for a deserted island in the Bahamas. Yes, we will have to change course now."

"What course now, sir? I will tell Hinze."

"Bring the sub to Bearing 270 and hold that heading; at each 10 hour interval, I want to be informed of our position."

"Yes sir," said Eric and informed Hinze of the new westerly heading.

As time and days slipped by, Captain Brunt began to feel the ship would never reach its planned destination. Fuel and food were running dangerously low and the crewmen were beginning to have doubts and fears over the decision they had made. It was now the 10th day since their decision to leave the war behind them.

Eric informed the Captain on this particular day that the ship was now "30-60". The fact that 30° N, 60° W indicated that they were now approaching the

'Devil's Triangle' had not gone unnoticed. Eric said, "I've read of this Devil's Triangle where ships disappear. Could it be this will be our fate? Will doom meet us here?"

Before Captain Brunt could answer, Schmidt shouted, "Contact! Ship – 10° to port!"

All anxiously awaited his next report, and in wonderment heard him say, "It appears to be circling, as if adrift. It shows to be over 60 feet in length but has no direction. It seems to be made of wood. Maybe an island schooner."

Captain Brunt decided to wait until nightfall. Around 1900, if all was clear, they would investigate further . . . providing the ship had not moved by then.

No movement was discerned throughout the waiting period, so at 1900 hours, Captain Brunt ordered the sub to surface. Once on the surface, the crewmen murmured over the very unusual sight; never before had they seen a ship drifting this far out at sea.

"Captain to engine room," said Brunt into the conning tower intercom.

"Yes, sir!" responded Rehrberg's voice.

"Proceed straight ahead, very slowly. We will try to tie her in as we come alongside her. Steady . . . good. All stop!"

Captain Brunt and Eric boarded the vessel, noticing no one on board. A meal, never eaten, was served on the table, but there was not a sign of life on board. "This is amazing, mysterious, and frightening to think about! Why should anyone abandon a good ship in such a hurry?" wondered Brunt.

"It does seem very strange," said Eric. "I noticed they have diesel engines, perhaps there is fuel aboard. We could surely use some if there is."

"You're right. Men, come aboard and strip the vessel of all usable material. Be careful in removing the fuel."

Once the ship was stripped clean, Brunt ordered her scuttled. The spirit of the U-237 crew rose sharply. There was additional fuel and additional food supplies as well. They could make the islands easily now, barring unforeseen disturbances.

Eric saved the ship's logs and once back aboard the sub his curiosity bade him to read the last entry — February 21,1937.

"February 21,1937: Proceeding as usual with weather calm and warm."

Then in the middle of the page was scrawled: "White water" nothing more. Eric became puzzled.

Schmidt interrupted Eric's train of thought by reporting to the Captain that the seaweed outside was getting thicker. "It might be better to run deeper, sir."

Eric said laughingly, "The Sargasso Sea. I wonder if we will stir the monsters."

Immediately Captain Brunt ordered, "Run at 60 feet, 15 knots until we clear the weeds, then notify me."

Eric sat with Captain Brunt over coffee in the dining area discussing the recent discovery of the abandoned ship. "Why had the ship been abandoned so hastily? What is 'White Water'? How could it cause the abandonment of a ship on an apparently calm, routine day? And why hasn't it been discovered within the past eight years? It doesn't make sense, Eric."

"I have heard of ships vanishing and being devoured by monsters but, of course, discredited all such accounts and assumed there had been other reasons for the disappearances. But I remember in Ulysses' account in the Odyssey there was mention of trouble they had with seaweed, but their ship survived and the men lived to tell the story. But none where the ship remained intact and the crew completely vanished."

"I wonder," said Captain Brunt, "if we have escaped one trouble just to get involved in another".

"We will just have to wait and see, Willie."

During the following week while everyone was busy on personal items, they were startled to hear the voice of Hinze booming over the intercom, "Captain, sir! I believe our compass is off . . . or we are somewhere 200 miles west of where I thought we were."

"Okay Hinze, I'll be right there. Let's see if we can get it squared away."

In the control room, all bearings were plotted again and checked out with known coordinates. Yet, on the periscope, there appeared an island, where the maps showed only open sea. The nearest island should have been 200 miles southwest of their current position.

"How is the seaweed situation at this moment, Hinze?" asked Brunt.

"We just cleared the area, sir," replied Hinze.

"Then take her up to periscope depth," ordered the Captain.

"Periscope depth, sir."

Brunt made a 360° sweep but in the darkness of the black night, little could be discerned. He then ordered a watch posted for the rest of the night with an alert to be called at sunup. All hands were then advised to get plenty of sleep for tomorrow might prove to be a taxing day!

"I wonder what we have found and where we really are?"

"What difference does it make, Willie, we are free and on top," replied Eric.

The following morning at 0650 hours, the alarm sounded and the sub came alive. All men were at their stations awaiting orders from the Captain. Willie wiped his face and nodded; the periscope was raised. After a complete 360° scan he began to plot the island. As he looked to the right side of the island, he noticed a light smoke which appeared to be moving on the island. Then a ship's bow cut into view. Brunt quickly slapped the turn handles up on the periscope and ordered, "Periscope down fast! Dive! Full Speed! Dive!"

At the same time Schmidt reported, "Cutter closing fast!"

"Take her to the bottom," ordered Brunt.

Again Schmidt broke in, "I have another ship closing on our starboard. Also one on our port, sir. Also the direction of the sub is heading us into the island, and there is rock surrounding it!"

"What is our depth?"

"184 feet, sir," reported Schmidt. "Bottom is 10 feet away."

Captain Brunt ordered, "All stop. All stop."

Rock seemed to be everywhere, surrounding the sub, almost completely enclosing it, when suddenly there appeared a break dead ahead; a narrow passage, a way out, but it would be close.

Brunt asked the navigator, "Calculate the passage width and see if the sub can pass through it safely."

"What about the ships, sir?" inquired Schmidt. "We can't read them because of all this rock."

"Good, that means they can't read us either."

"Sir! We are drifting into the channel as if being pulled. My instruments! Look at them! The gauges are all going crazy — the needles are spinning wildly around in circles!" cried Hinze.

"Take it easy, Hinze. Quiet and listen."

Every once in a while the sub would rub against the rocks; then the sub stopped and appeared to bounce.

"Do you feel it now? It's like we are tied up at dock. All quiet!" ordered Brunt. "Give me a reading from the depth gauge Schmidt."

"It registers surface level, sir! Are we on the surface?"

"Give me a foot on the periscope," said the Captain, as he reached to his left and began to press his eye to the viewer.

"I can't believe it! I just can't believe it! Give a look here, Eric."

Eric took over the periscope and gasped at the sight before him. "We are surrounded by an eerie greenish light. The sub seems to have surfaced in some kind of cave. That would explain our depth level gauge registering surface. The pressure here is similar to what we would experience travelling at surface level. Amazing!"

"Down scope!" bellowed Brunt as he contemplated their next move. "Send Carl Rehrberg to me."

Carl entered the control room in response to the Captain's request. "Yes, sir?"

"I want you to enter the double chamber with an oxygen bottle. Open the outside hatch and see if there is oxygen here for us to breathe."

As Carl closed the inner hatch behind him and then started opening the outer hatch door, he noticed a musty smell creeping in to meet him. The air was cool and he discovered that he could breathe quite well in spite of the musty odor. He tapped on the inner hatch and began unscrewing the lid. There was a moment of silence and anxiety below while waiting for Rehrberg to tell them what the situation appeared to be.

"Come on out," invited Carl, "the weather's fine."

As everyone began to emerge, the emerald-like color coming from the channel entrance under the water gave each one a ghostly appearance. They looked around, and as their eyes grew accustomed to the light, their wonderment grew. They had surfaced inside a cave-like underwater chamber, yet there was no water inside the chamber. It was like an air pocket of some kind . . . but how did it remain like this?

"Where are we?" Carl inquired. "Hey! Look over there! Those standing columns! They look as if they're made of marble! They're beautiful!"

Eric had a strange desire to inspect everything. He wanted to examine the columns at a closer range and requested the gang-plank be placed down. He then proceeded to make a careful evaluation of their situation. It appeared that the sub was berthed in a channel of water approximately 30 feet wide and 100 feet long. He judged the cave-like room surrounding the sub to be approximately 28 feet high, 153 feet long and 50 feet wide, with the marble columns placed every ten feet around the room. Eric cautiously entered the chamber and found himself standing on a marble deck. Looking around, he noticed openings in the walls which looked like doors; all leading off in a different direction. Mounted on the South wall, or built into the wall, was a strange face-like object approximately three feet in diameter, with red eyes, and rays encircling it resembling ancient representations of the Sun God. Eric's eyes were growing more accustomed to seeing in the green haze, and noticed the strange writings on the wall. It must be some sort of hieroglyphics, he thought. Then he searched his mind for long-forgotten recollections from his ancient history studies. Perhaps he could, in some way, explain what kind of structure they had discovered. Suddenly Eric knew.

"We must be in a sunken pyramid!" he exclaimed. "If I'm right, this will be a priceless discovery dating back thousands of years! All men back to the sub!"

Once re-assembled in the sub, Eric explained further. "It may be we have stumbled upon a very old and unique structure. It could crumble at any time. However, I would like a few specially trained men to accompany me so we can complete a full survey. I want to measure and examine the entire room with very delicate care. Rehrberg, Schmidt, Hinze, will you help me?"

"Of course, sir," they answered in unison.

The remaining crewmen busied themselves in the sub while the exploration party began to formulate their plans. To orient themselves, they judged their direction from the last reading that had been taken. The heading was Southwest, so they judged the right rear to be the Northwest corner and began their explorations from there.

After assembling their measuring equipment, they began to meticulously survey the entire room. To their amazement they found that the doors were spaced precisely at fifty-one foot intervals. Along the walls were discovered writings, and various drawings carved into the walls . . . even a stone tablet with writing on it.

Eric asked Rehrberg, "Go back and get Heinrich Goulstchat. Tell him to bring his sketching pad and pens." Eric wanted accurate detailed representations of all the writings and drawings for further study.

After supper that evening, Eric established a headquarters for himself in the Captain's stateroom. He needed additional space to spread out the drawings Heinrich had made so he could compare them more closely. He discovered some symbols to be identical, while others were unique . . . while yet others closely resembled more symbols but were not exactly the same.

Several of the designs were unanimous in their reference to North and South as in poles of a magnetic field. Each human form contained a magnetic field around it — like a glow. One form was lying prone, while the other seemed to be waving his hand over him. More than once, reference was made by a symbolic lightning bolt.

The writings were almost Hebraic in form, which really took Eric back to his early years recalling his ability to translate.

One such writing began with

ש ל גנ ד ד ח כ ש . . .

which when fully translated Eric found it to mean, "The body has two magnetic fields which control the body fluids. When the fluids are in balance, the body is efficient; when the fluids are upset, the person is usually ill. To balance these fluids, all one had to do is have someone rub their hands together until they are warm, then with one hand travel from head to toe, two inches from the surface of the body."

Next came,

ש כ ח ד נ ש

. . . Eric began to fully interpret, "The mind is both conscious and unconscious in existence. The unconscious mind controls the overall action of the individual. Always in a commanding or repairing phase, like an alarm within the system. Completely controlled in a conscious manner, the unconscious can be projected to others; to control others; just as we are controlling you now."

Almost in a daze, Eric sat and read, "In the next few hours your system will become completely responsive to thoughts of others. You, by thought, can get their attention, have them relax, and convey your wishes to them. Now you will close your eyes and relax, deeper, now relax all over, let your toes relax, your legs, now your arms, your entire body, relax . . . ," Eric dozed off.

He awoke with a start at 0500 hours and realized just how everything fit together. After breakfast was finished, he gathered the men around him and explained his theory to them.

"Men, my best guess is that we have discovered a tomb, or pyramid, as the old kings called them. Some natural catastrophe occurring in ages past trapped this room and probably some others under the sea — like a diving bell or a bowl upside down in the water. How the air remains fresh in here I haven't yet been able to understand, but perhaps there are clues we can piece together to help explain such a phenomenon. I believe we have discovered an ancient wonder of the world, complete with many secrets and mysteries. The key to the secrets here will probably be found in the deciphering and translating of the ancient wall writings into things we can understand. It may be that our world will discover many secrets of the ancient world from this cave . . including perhaps the lost city of Atlantis."

The men's conversation buzzed. Questions, theories, conjectures, all flew in every direction.

"Would you answer some questions, if you can Doctor?" asked one crewman.

"I will answer as best I can at this moment," he replied. "There are still many questions that I have myself."

"Can you tell us for sure what direction we're facing?"

"I'm sure the room is set in a pure North-South direction."

"Do you think there is any way we can get on top of the dome?" questioned Brunt.

"Do we have any scuba gear on board?" asked Eric.

"Yes, there is some stowed away in my cabin. An entire set for two men. Brought along in case we needed outside repairs."

"Good," responded Eric enthusiastically, "Maybe we can use it today. I'll also need all the crewmen in the 'green room' today. We are going to try and pinpoint the source of the air ingress."

With their course of action clear, all men were eager to get to their assigned posts in the chamber. Eric insisted that no one was to venture close to the doorways; just remain stationed throughout the vast cave at given intervals and try to find cracks or any possible openings that would allow air to enter the area.

Eric requested Herman Kofcher, one of the instrument men aboard, to make a staff gauge to see if the water rose or fell. As each man set about his task, it resembled an Eskimo egg hunt; all crewmen were bundled up warmly as the temperature was a steady 42° Fahrenheit, with a dampness in the air that chilled their bones.

Everyone was busy feeling and scanning the walls when a crewman, Johan Vandel, a chemist by trade, discovered air entering through the eyes of "the face with tear drops."

"Here it is, sir!" he shouted to Eric. "Air is coming in through these eyes."

The crew immediately gathered around Johan at the 'face'. Previous measurements had revealed the structure to be exactly 28.28 inches in diameter, and a perfect circle. The two three-inch eyes were round rubies; it was here Johan discovered the air blowing in. Eric depressed one eye very gently discovering it moved easily in and out, cutting off the supply of air when depressed.

"Check this out, Herman," Eric told Kofcher. "Rig up some sort of measuring device to check the pressure at half-hour intervals. I'd be interested in knowing if it is constant or if it changes periodically. Keep a log and see if a pattern can be discerned."

Hans Ribtoff, the first officer, had been assigned to survey the left part of the North wall. Upon passing a doorway, he thought he could see metal resembling a large drive shaft. "Doctor, look here! I've found some sort of metal structure about 3 feet in diameter with flat areas on each side which look like shelves." Hans then reached in his pocket for his knife but it dropped to the floor as he took it from his pocket. All the crewmen watched as the knife began to slide toward the large rod. Hans reached out to attempt its retrieval.

"STOP HANS!" ordered Eric. "Don't go near the doorway!"

The warning came too late as Hans made contact with his knife. A huge spark lit him up from head to toe. By the time he hit the floor, he was burned black.

"Do not touch him. Everyone stand clear!" commanded Eric. "I told you to avoid going near the doorways! There is a strong power, unknown to us yet, which resides behind the doors. You must all stay clear!"

Eric summoned Johan, the chemist, along with Herman Kofcher and Peter Loftin, both of whom were instrument specialists, to a conference. "We must try to discover the cause of Hans's death. Also we must try to devise a safe method of removing his body without risking contamination ourselves."

Just then Captain Brunt joined the conference. "I must insist on one thing right now. All of us must get out of this room and back to the submarine. I don't care if we ever discover the secrets of this pyramid! I just cannot allow more men to die! What good will it do mankind for us to have made this discovery if all of us are dead before we can reach anyone with our information? I insist we leave this entire area immediately!"

"Your reasoning is sound Willie," declared Eric. "Just let me have twenty-four more hours for further study; then I agree, we should leave."

CHAPTER III

In order to retrieve Han's body, Johan, Peter and Herman devised two insulated poles to pull the corpse from the death area. While working with one of the poles, an eight inch chip was knocked off the mysterious rod which Johan pulled to the opening.

As Eric observed the chip being retrieved, he asked, "Do you know if we have any dead batteries on board, Carl?"

"Yes sir, we do." Carl answered.

"Let's try something with this. Bring me one of them, Carl."

The battery was brought and a dead cell removed from the case and replaced with the chip of rod they had just recovered.

Peter asked, "Why not get a chip from the rod used on the other side of the doorway and place it in the other end of the battery case?"

As Johan walked over to the other rod, he remarked, "Hans had taken samples of the water here and it contained acid. Let's use some of it in the case before we seal it."

Eric added, "According to the information I deciphered from the tablet, the case should be reconstructed to resemble a pyramid with the poles lined on true North and South. Then it will create an electromagnetic field; in this sense, with the battery exposed to the sun, it will build lumers, and each lumer will build watts."

Carl said, "In other words, exposure to the sun will cause the ultra-violet rays to increase the wattage of our battery. It will continue to work forever. Theoretically speaking, we would have perpetual power!"

Peter followed with, "We are being exposed to a similar force right now, Carl. Static electricity has set the force in motion. I just can't understand why a chain reaction didn't develop."

Eric responded, "The pyramid is constant, immovable; thus the reaction is low until the ultra-violet rays build up, then it comes alive and causes a magnetic storm of great magnitude."

"But," Peter said, "who built a pyramid here and why?"

Eric surmised, "The powers that were, called Ancients, built pyramids according to very precise specifications and plans as you saw from our measurements. I believe their ships came with instructions for constructing the pyramids, which then became beacons for navigational control. It was probably years after their completed construction, when the planet began to die. The crying face could have been left as consolation for the remaining inhabitants after all the escape voyages possible had been made."

"The chips, acid and water are all together now. I believe the battery is complete," said Peter.

"Fasten the top securely." Eric instructed, "but do not touch the poles . . . We do not know how powerful it is."

Jack Schindler was given the task of removing Han's body. A plan they thought might work had Jack placing the remains in a rubber bag by the use of the poles. Jack slipped on the green slime, touching the body as he fell. The intense pain from the shock received when he touched it caused him to call out to Eric. "Doctor! Please, my hands are burning! What should I do?"

Eric, looking despondent, said to Carl, "Get the battery on board." Then shouted to the crew, "All personnel are directed to take a shower as soon as possible. The force is still too strong for us to recover the body . . . we will have to leave it."

"You mean we are being exposed to radioactivity right now? Are we being mumified?" queried Carl.

"Yes, Carl. We must leave and at once! Quickly, get some water! Douse Jack with all you can find," shouted Eric.

By now Jack's skin was turning black as he

screamed from the intense pain.

"What can we do now, sir?" Peter asked almost hysterically.

"Nothing! The radiation is much stronger than I expected. Jack . . . make your peace with God."

Jack fell in agony. Soon though, his agony was over . . . the pain gone . . . he lay dead on the marble floor. All the men began filing out with Eric the last to leave the chamber. As he pulled the hatch door closed behind him, he wondered what could have been done to save Jack? Anything? He hated the thought of being the cause of another's death. Could it have been prevented or was it part of some plan revealed in the writings and not yet deciphered? Eric secured the hatch, closing out the greenish light from the chamber and the tomb forever.

Captain Brunt said, "We must submerge in place at least twenty feet. We will then set our dive for 400 feet, and as soon as we are out of the chamber, we will come to 184 feet. All stations ready?"

"Yes sir, all stations ready and manned."

"Very well. Dive!" commanded Brunt. "Call off the depth, Schmidt."

"Yes sir. We are now diving . . . 30 feet, . . . 60 feet, . . . 100 feet, . . . 200 feet, . . . 300 feet, . . . 400 feet, sir"

"Reverse engines. Slow."

The hull began to rub on the rock corridor. "Come to 184 feet," said Brunt.

"290 feet, sir . . . 220 feet, . . . 184 feet," called Schmidt, as the grinding became heavier.

"Full speed," replied the Captain.

The grinding became continuous now as the ship began to level and move backward faster and faster.

"We're clearing the rocks now, sir. Clear now," a relieved Schmidt reported.

"All stop. Surface to periscope depth," ordered Brunt.

"Periscope depth, sir," reported Schmidt. "Sonar/Radar clear."

As Captain Brunt scanned the horizon, the sun

was low in the West with less than an hour before sunset. "We will sit calm and wait until darkness falls. Eric, will you accompany me to my quarters?"

Eric and the Captain sat, neither saying anything for a long while. Then the Captain began.

"We have come this far to get out of danger, to find peace, to be free and start a new life. But it appears we are back where we started. We have made no progress at all, and only heaven knows what kind of danger we face from here on. What's the use?"

Eric sat quietly for a moment longer. Then turning towards Brunt, said, "As long as we live, we live with death. As long as we search for peace, we will never find it. But never finding it doesn't mean we will never be free. I must tell you Willie, we have found the secret to peace and to freedom. It is up to us to use it. The Ancients, the powers that came to this planet, mixed into our evolution. In other words, brought intelligence to an ape-man. Today, we have a mixture of ape-man and intelligent being. Which will win out? They tell us that man, the Son of Dust, will rule the planet Earth, but the heavens will be ruled by the intelligent. There are some men who feel the heavenly spirit of intelligence and know peace and love. From the tablet I learned why we must love, must be at peace. I know this force loves and creates peace, and can be great and good or it can be so tremendously evil. Man must learn to live without envy or greed. The world needs to be free from want and desire. Man must love his fellow man. Otherwise, he will destroy the planet Earth."

Brunt said, "I saw what happened to Hans and Jack. Is this force you speak of the cause of their destruction?"

Thoughtfully, Eric replied, "No. The force is man's mind. The power comes from the sun and gives man energy; man's mind does the rest. When this alien race arrived here at their destination, they could transfer thoughts to the inhabitants with no need for words or other forms of communications. They always realized their desires by using thought transference. Just think what the world would be like today without the concepts of love and peace we inherited from that race. What would man dream of or conceive now if there wasn't this force?"

"Eric, do you really believe these alien people could get what they wanted by this thought transfer method you talk about? Do you believe they could levitate great stones or other objects? How do you suppose they traveled here . . . flying carpets!!!"

"I'm afraid so, Willie," answered Eric, "they could move about at will. They had, you know, achieved great power but then lost it. As their original blood line passed down through generations, it was mixed with blood of lesser beings. Man, of Earth, became intelligent but lacked common sense. It is man's thirst to know God which brings us to our present situation."

"You mean, after all this, you now say there is a God? You believe in God, Eric?"

"Yes, and I believe his power is stronger than all powers."

"I never thought I'd hear you say that!" Brunt said. "Next you will marry a Jewish girl!"

"With that remark, I will retire," Eric said. "It's been a tiring day, but first I want this position marked. By the way, what day is it now?"

"May 5, 1945," answered Brunt, reaching for the intercom. "Schmidt, mark the position of this island, please."

"Yes sir. North 28°, West 77.5°. I've marked it, sir."

"Has the radio been repaired yet, Schmidt?"

"No, Captain. There is still interference. I can't determine what the trouble is."

Eric suggested, "The first chance we get, sand the antennae to reduce the effect of the electromagnetic field they were in. The problem will probably disappear. It's as if they have been chrome-plated."

CHAPTER IV

0530 hours the next morning found all hands up and about as soon as the first bell sounded. There was a feeling of great anticipation in the air as the crew was anxious to feel firm ground under their feet again, and with any luck they should find their new world today. Captain Brunt ordered the sub to proceed to periscope depth around the island, taking soundings on the sonar as they went.

"It seems, sir, as though there is an inlet, or bay of some kind, on the East side," reported Schmidt. And as the navigator maneuvered the craft into the passage remarked, "Area clear, sir. No ships or other activity on the horizon."

"Surface!" ordered the Captain. "Ensign Durbin report to me at once."

When Paul Durbin appeared, the Captain directed him to get into his diving gear and make a reconnaissance trip around the lagoon. "If the reconnaissance tour proves the situation to be safe, you are instructed to tie up the sub. Then you will proceed to explore the island on foot."

The presence of thick mangrove and sea grapes seemed to be a good omen to Brunt. Besides providing shelter and beauty, there would be fresh fruit. He remembered reports of the delicate flavor of the sea grape berries from sailors who had traveled to the tropics before the war. The island might prove to be a paradise!

"All stop!" ordered Brunt. "The situation here seems to be good, but I recommend we proceed with due caution. First, I need several men to cover the deck with leaves and brush to conceal our presence. Then, we will proceed in small groups to help Paul explore the island. We will all meet back here at 0730 hours sharp and pool our findings. In case of trouble of any sort, a shrill whistle will bring help from all nearby. Now let's see how some solid ground feels to our sea legs!"

"May I sand my antennae off as Dr. von Wilhelm suggested, sir? My equipment is still not working properly and this seems a good time to work on it," queried Schmidt.

"All right Schmidt, but work quickly as possible. We may have to leave here unexpectedly . . . and in a hurry!"

"What did you find on the antenna, Schmidt?" asked Eric as they stood on the deck together watching the men disperse.

"Something resembling a white rust, sir. They're clear now though. Just a light covering of some sort," replied Schmidt as he went back into the sub to his radio and sonar position.

Suddenly over the radio came a news flash reporting that Germany had surrendered. Schmidt ran to the deck of the sub and shouted to the Captain. "Sir! Sir! Come listen!"

Brunt and those within earshot ran speedily back to the sub and quickly assembled around the radio. As they listened, they stood silent. The news of the surrender was followed by a report that the Russians had taken control of the country. Germany had fallen. The crew was sad but grateful that they were on an island thousands of miles away. Their homeland was no longer theirs. They had made their best decision when they quit the war; no German sailor could live under the Russians—it was better to be free, trying to start anew.

Later, the soothing water of the bay was a welcome relief to those who plunged in, lessening their depression from the earlier news as they swam or lay on the beach . . . their bodies soaking up the sunshine. And as they did so, one survey group returned to report that they had discovered an old pirate's well with fresh cool water.

"We have all we need, Captain . . . all except for food and love!" shouted Oscar Hiney.

A week went by without incident. Everyone had enjoyed the sun, the soft blue water, the excellent meals that Hiney prepared, and even the work which was required for survival, for it was accomplished in clean fresh air. Eric seized the opportunity to continue his studies on mind control by practicing on the crew daily.

The serenity was broken a few days later. Paul Durbin, while on watch duty, shouted below, "We're being visited. Ship sighted entering the bay at two o'clock!"

Cutting a wake into the bay came a U.S. Navy PT Boat which anchored not more than fifty yards away, and as the crew of the sub sat quiet, the PT Boat crew began to swim, fish and relax, having no idea that the island was inhabited. As night fell, the boat still remained at anchor.

"Willie," Eric said, "we must capture the American boat. It's the same as being on the bottom, this way."

"I see your point, Eric. We will make plans to overtake the PT Boat crew later tonight."

The plan was set in motion at 2100 hours. A boarding party was sent to overcome the crew without violence. Quietly everyone, except the Captain, Eric, Hinze, and Hiney, boarded the PT Boat. However, they were discovered and the next moment brought machine gun fire followed by silence. Then the crew of the PT Boat were brought aboard the sub as captives. Carl hesitatingly reported five of their men had lost their lives to the American machine gunner.

Captain Brunt ordered the captured men locked below deck. "It was needless for those men to die," Captain Brunt said, throwing his cap to the floor. "Report – who was shot."

Carl began, "Olaf, Edward, Carl Swenson, Rudolph and Hector."

"Damn it! Hang the one who did it!" Brunt shouted.

Eric spoke up, "Hold it, Willie! We will suffer our loss. I can now turn these American's minds back in time so they will never remember tonight. In this way, we can arrange for them to bring us fresh supplies. Just give me time . . . it won't take long."

"I agree that we need supplies . . . but damn it, Eric, if you fail, I'll hang them all!"

After a moment of concentration on deck, Eric went below and began talking to the captured crew. Within thirty-five minutes all were in a hypnotic trance being taken deeper and deeper. Finally Eric began the regression in time that brought them to the minute just before the raid. He then reprogrammed their minds to erase the memory of the raid and bloodshed, and at the same time, implanted the suggestion to the PT crew that they would return to the island with supplies for the sub, although they would have no memory of the transaction. The gathering and loading of supplies and the trip to sea would happen but not be remembered. Eric's final instructions to the sailors were, "Now get the list of needed supplies as fast as you can and return here to us."

As one of the sailors passed Oscar, he said jokingly, "Bring some women with you when you come back . . . about 18 to 20 years old. Find us some real pretty girls."

The American sailors returned to the PT Boat, and with supply list in hand, weighed anchor and left the island.

"Eric, I hope this works for all our sakes. Well, we will worry later. Now let's get about the task of burying our friends. We will have to row out and bury them at sea. We will begin the funeral preparations right now."

So the next few hours, the crew of the U-237 buried their dead. Later that evening, at 2100 hours, Eric emerged from his room and went to the Captain's quarters. He had been reviewing the tablet writings, the battery, and the survey crew's measurements of the green room. From what Eric learned in the writings he had brought himself to full rest, whispered "ALPHA" and then proceeded to the Captain's stateroom.

As soon as Eric entered, Oscar brought two cups of coffee. Eric had experienced his first successful thought transference!

"Oscar, I didn't send for coffee."

"No Willie, I did," said Eric. "And yes, Captain, the PT Boat will be back at 2200 hours tonight." As if in a trance, Eric continued, "A power meeting is scheduled for someone here on Earth. Someone in space is due to make contact."

Brunt said, "What are you talking about, Eric? When is what supposed to make contact? With who?"

Eric responded, "The answer is contained in the dimensions of the pyramids; it relates to their position and location, and indicates which sector of the sky the contact will either come from or to which part one of us should go."

"What do you mean? One of us go up to heaven?"

"It is very vague now, but it's possible the powers intend that someone here, go there."

Peter then knocked on the door, opened it slightly and asked, "Did someone here call me? I just received a strong urge to come here. I feel weird!"

"Yes Peter, I asked you to come," said Eric. "Your keen mind can be of help to us now."

"How did you call me?"

"It was a message transmitted by thought transference, which I have accomplished. In time, you will understand. For now, I'm interested mainly in your reaction to what we discovered; meaning the pyramid, green room, tablet, and the rest. What do you think about it?"

"Doctor, the air in the tomb? Where did it come from?"

"I've been trying to figure out just that for days; how the fresh air is kept in circulation. I think I can answer that now. You remember the eyes moved in and out? They let the fresh air in and the pressure that is created keeps the chamber from collapsing. Picture a tall structure on either side of the pyramid, with the top higher than the surrounding ocean waters, thus open to the air. A tunnel connects these structures and passes the pyramid at the level where the eyes of the 'crying face' are built. On top of one of these tall structures is a mass of reflective material which captures the sun's rays and causes temperatures to build up between 500 and 1000 degrees Fahrenheit. This great concentration of heat draws the air already in the pyramid up and out creating an air transfer in the tunnel. Wind whistles through the tunnel at 100 miles per hour, allowing the air to circulate into the chamber. When this wind force is passing through the tunnel, the eyes remain closed which maintains the chamber's pressure. It's a very ingenious plan; you saw for yourself it really works! A profound discovery . . . remarkable! We have obtained some very significant information from this underground pyramid."

"No matter. Now we must be more practical and plan our town," Brunt suggested. "This theorizing is very interesting, but I think we have more important matters which must be given our attention."

"I think the best location for a settlement would be on the high terrain and close to a well. We can use the mangrove trees for cover," suggested Peter.

Eric's trance somewhat broken by the interruption said, "Yes, go ahead with the plans and construction. It will keep the men gainfully occupied."

"May we begin now, sir?"

"Yes, Peter, go ahead," Captain Brunt replied and Eric nodded.

Later that evening, nearing 2200 hours, Captain Brunt queried Schmidt. "Can you see anything on radar?"

"No sir, not yet . . . I will report as soon as it arrives, sir."

Around 2230 hours, Schmidt reported to the Captain. "The ship is in, sir. I have alerted the crew and they are assembled on deck."

All were amazed to see the PT Boat pull right up to the rear of the sub. When it was secured, Eric instructed the men to begin unloading the cases of meat, fresh vegetables, canned goods, and tobacco. Unknown to anyone but Oscar, a sailor deposited two large sacks apart from the others. Then before the PT Boat left, Eric suggested that they return in a week with additional stores.

Oscar placed all his supplies in the bins, and without notice, slipped out to where the two sacks had been placed. Upon opening the first sack, Oscar knew he was in trouble. Inside there was a girl in her late teens, gagged and tied, and with tears rolling down her pretty face. He immediately opened the second and found another young girl inside, possibly twenty years old, with long black hair and dark eyes, similarly tied and gagged. Oscar was at a complete loss. "Oh God," he said, "what in the world am I going to do with these girls? Why did I tell him to bring them?"

Oscar went immediately for Carl. When Carl returned with Oscar and saw the two girls, his first reaction was, "Oh! They're beautiful! I haven't seen one for so long!" Then the danger of their presence entered his mind and he realized what a problem they really were. "Oscar, take one sack and I'll take the other. We'll go up to the shacks . . . there's one that is nearly finished. We can hide them there for awhile."

Once at the new town they were building, they entered the nearly completed shack. Carl gently put the youngest girl down and removed her ties and gag. She began to cry, speaking between sobs, "Where am I? What happened?"

Carl didn't know how to handle this and Oscar was scared out of his senses. He wondered if he'd ever risk a joke again! Oscar unfastened the other girl's ties and gag and she immediately spoke up. "What's this all about? Why are we here? I demand to know what's happening! I'm supposed to be at work right now! Where am I?" Then noticing how upset the other girl was, she tried to comfort her. "It won't help to cry. What's your name?"

"Nancy. What's yours?"

"Sheila. Now calm down, Nancy. This could be worse. Let's see what develops."

Then Carl said, "Please be quiet and get some sleep. No one will bother you, I promise."

The girls were so exhausted and over-wrought they could not get comfortably arranged on the hard dirt floor.

Carl stood guard outside for the rest of the night to insure that no one would get to the girls while Oscar went back to the sub.

In the morning, Eric was the first one up, looking for a cup of coffee. When he noticed Oscar's erratic behavior, he asked, "All right Oscar, what is it?"

Oscar started, "I'm sorry. I meant it as a joke, but it was taken seriously."

"I told the American sailors to bring us some women the other night. They did! There are two girls up on the hill now and I don't know what to do about them? I'm sorry, Doctor von Wilhelm. It was a joke."

Eric sat quietly for a moment, wondering what to do next. "Get Captain Brunt."

"What now!" shouted Brunt as he came through the doorway.

Eric relayed to him what happened and they agreed that it was necessary to countermand any sexual drives the crew might have. Chaos would result if the presence of females was discovered.

Right after breakfast all hands were called together and Eric transferred to each and every one present a suggestion designed to subdue their sexual drives. He then went to the shack where the girls were being kept.

Carl was still asleep outside the shack and did not even waken as Eric stepped over him and entered the room. The two girls were huddled together and Eric saw the two slender shapes cower as he approached them. One had long straight black hair and the other curly blonde hair, cut short and very becoming to the pixie-like face it surrounded. A protective feeling arose in him as he quietly said to the girls, "Don't be afraid."

Each girl's eyes held terror in them. They closed them as if they were afraid to look at him. They held tight to each other in mortal fear for their lives.

"Please, I won't hurt you. I am the ship's doctor. Are you both all right?"

The girls relaxed somewhat and let loose of each other. Sheila spoke first. "I'm fine. But what's going on? One minute I'm going to work and then the next I'm grabbed by a sailor, tied up, put in a dirty old bag, and handled like a sack of potatoes. The next thing I know I'm in a boat and end up here. Now tell me . . . what's going on? Where am I?"

Eric explained, "A tragic mistake has been made. You two are prisoners for the moment, but by tomorrow night you will be on your way home again, safe and sound, never to remember any of this. I will send some food up to you, okay?" Then going outside, "Get up Carl! You've overslept. Bring these girls something to eat, a hot meal, and don't let anyone see you."

Eric later told the Captain, "We need to post guards on the girls until they can be sent home. It isn't safe to leave them unguarded while there are so many men around."

"Why Eric? You gave them the suggestion to curb their sex drives, didn't you?"

"Yes, I did. But without moral intelligence it may be useless . . . it may not have worked."

"Very well, we will post guards. Who would you suggest?"

"How about Carl and Oscar? They're the only ones who know about the girls now and I hope it stays that way. I'm sure the suggestion will remain in force on them; it's some of these other men I just can't be sure about."

The day continued on without incident. Carl brought the girls their meals and enjoyed sitting and talking to them. He learned that Nancy was eighteen and interested mainly in finding a husband and starting a family. Sheila, though, had more serious plans for her life. As a full-time lab technician and part-time student, she hoped to go into medical research upon receiving her diploma. For the present, all thoughts of a husband and family were far from her mind.

Oscar had the first evening guard shift since he had to be up early to prepare breakfast. He had been extremely busy during the day and very tired. Around 2200 hours he became drowsy and began to doze off. ZAP! A flash of lights before his eyes and a feeling of sudden pain and then nothing . . . Oscar fell forward from the blow to the top of his head.

Two of the crewmen, Schoft and Frederich, had knocked Oscar unconscious . . . Eric's suggestion not taking root in their sub-conscious. Intent on gaining possession of the women, they had followed Oscar up to the shack with plans of their own . . . to have a real big night with the girls.

Schoft went into the shack first and told the girls they would have to be moved to a different location for their safety and asked them to be very quiet.

"Did Doctor von Wilhelm send you?" asked Sheila.

"Sure!" replied Schoft with a grin on his face.

Willingly the girls accompanied them to the other side of the island. There they were gagged and bound again, Sheila yelling for help just before they could get her gag secured.

Frederich gave her face a hard sharp slap. "Shut up woman! We're going to have some fun with you two . . . and we don't want any one disturbing us."

They then began savagely tearing off the girls' clothes, reducing them to shreds of cloth scattered over the ground. Lust which filled their hearts was reflected in their eyes, over-riding any decent or human thoughts. They were existing on a primitive animal-like level with their bodies and not their minds in control.

Once the girls had been stripped naked, their bodies now racking with great sobs, and tears streaming down their faces, the greedy passion which ruled the men as they viewed the two young bodies before them, took over their senses. They lunged with brutal force at the girls, knocking them to the ground where they fought for release from their sexual desires.

With their first rush of passion fulfilled, the men lay in the grass laughing and joking about their conquests. The girls, crouched near some rocks trying to hide their nakedness and crying softly, were attempting to comfort each other.

Shortly, Frederich walked over to Nancy, and as she tried to get away from him, he struck her with a fierce blow to her curly blonde head. Sheila knew by the way that Nancy fell that her neck was broken, but Frederich was unaware of anything but his own lust and desire. He clawed at her already bruised and bleeding body, but there was no longer any resistance.

Schoft, meanwhile, had turned his attention to Sheila and began tearing at her long black hair. Her body went slack and her eyes became listless, as there was no strength left in her to fight. The cruel rape continued until the men, now completely spent, rolled over on their backs in exhaustion, completely sated.

It was this disheveled scene that Carl discovered moments later. He had gone to relieve Oscar on guard duty only to find Oscar still unconscious and the shack empty. He rushed to several other shacks on which construction had begun but found no one. Then he ran to the other side of the island, and once there and saw what had happened, knew he was too late to help.

Nancy's skin was now a greyish color under the streaks of dried blood. Sheila was deathly pale with claw marks, bite marks and ugly scrape markings covering her entire body. Schoft and Frederich lay in an exhausted state, snoring loudly.

Carl's heart sank. To think such cruelty was possible. He couldn't believe his fellow crewmen could be so savage. As he viewed this ravaged scene he was joined by Oscar who had finally recovered from the knock-out blow and was searching for the girls.

"What can we do, Carl?"

"We must get Eric here immediately," Carl answered. "You stand guard here. I'll return with him in just a minute."

A short time later, the three men stood and surveyed the situation. Full of rage, Carl said, "First we should hang Schoft and Frederich, or shoot them to death. They don't deserve to live anymore."

Eric knelt down beside Nancy and examined her. "She's dead," he said slowly. "Her neck is broken. Either that or this large gash in her head killed her."

"What about Sheila?" Carl asked.

Eric began wiping the blood from her face as he felt for her pulse. Faintly he heard the pulse . . . weak but steady.

"Quickly! We must cover her and cleanse her wounds. She is still alive!"

Immediately Oscar ran for a blanket, while Eric worked on her badly bruised body. Carl was instructed to make a stretcher so she could be safely carried to the Doctor's quarters aboard the sub.

"We must bury Nancy . . . but first I will deal with Schoft and Frederich. Take Sheila to the sub at once and when you return start to dig a grave for Nancy. I will take care of these beasts here and now. Wake up Schoft! Frederich! Come to attention!"

Their stupor left at the sound of von Wilhelm's command and they responded at once.

Eric addressed them directly, saying, "Your behavior has reduced you two to a level below that of animals in a jungle. Since you have behaved like mad dogs, you will die like mad dogs. Since you are so sex-minded, you are now going to experience continual orgasms until you are dead. Sexual satisfaction is all that is in your minds. Now begin!"

Eric knew that this suggestion would take . . . not only because they were acceptable to this kind of suggestion but because he had applied his complete concentration to their minds.

Immediately each man fell to the ground. Schoft began to jerk and moan, then Frederich. Both men lay on the ground jerking and moaning as Eric left them to their fate.

Carl, returning with a shovel, surveyed the scene and realizing what was happening, screamed, "Doctor! You are going to kill them!"

Eric never stopped. He proceeded to the sub and informed Captain Brunt of the situation he had encountered and the steps he had taken to rectify it. He then went to his quarters and began administering medical aid to Sheila.

Later, Eric, Captain Brunt and Carl returned to the far side of the island and found both men dead. Eric commanded Carl to drag them to the ocean's edge so the crabs could pick them clean.

Nancy's body, which had been wrapped in the blanket, was then placed in the grave and Captain Brunt commended her spirit to heaven. Then the three saddened men returned to the sub.

CHAPTER V

The next several weeks found all crew members busy completing their town. Eric continued his studies while trying to help Sheila recover from the physical wounds; her mind being still in deep shock.

Captain Brunt entered Eric's quarters. "Eric, it has been a while since Sheila's ordeal. Is her condition improving?"

"No. I haven't been able to reach her mind yet. Oscar is preparing some bone marrow soup – considered to be brain food – in an attempt to reach her."

"Why bone marrow?"

"It has always been thought that vampires needed blood; actually they were after bone marrow. It is the energy giving substance needed to retain a high degree of concentration. During daylight hours, ultraviolet rays eat up this energy from the body. That's why I have only been going out evenings."

"Sounds like you've turned into a Hyde, Doctor," quipped Brunt laughingly.

"I am trying to get my energy level up, as I'll need all I can muster to handle Sheila and the Americans. Also I have been receiving vibrations of thought that an awesome event will occur around the middle of July. You know, if this pyramid is upset I do not know what the result will be. We must prepare."

"Very well, Eric. Give me your plan if you have one."

"That's the problem. I don't have any. I won't know what to do until it happens."

The next morning Eric concentrated on Sheila to bring her around. As he began, a feeling of great tiredness overcame him but Sheila began to respond. She became fully awake and calm as Eric kept suggesting she would never remember Nancy or the horrible incident of that night on the beach. By this time Eric was exhausted, however Sheila, intuitively, sensed his need and she immediately began to help him.

In the days to come Sheila became his assistant and even helped him to interpret the tablets. Seeing how well Sheila was recovering made Captain Brunt wonder if it wasn't all part of some grand scheme that she had to suffer . . . to be practically reborn. He also wondered why those two men had killed the girl and raped both her and Sheila.

"Eric, I have been overly-curious as to why Shoft and Frederich attacked the two girls. Is there any sane reasoning behind it?"

"Willie, this is the same story the ancients speak of. Immoral and unintelligent beings began to use their power to control and run things the way they wanted. This caused a disruption to their normal way of life. No woman was safe. Sometimes gangs of men or grown boys would capture a woman and rape her and then leave her to die. The society degenerated, family life split up, and the monetary system became impossible to maintain. The ancients felt a total annihilation of the known world was in order . . . so Atlantis was destroyed. This is written on the tablet that we found below . . . thus, when we speak of present day witches, fortune tellers, or anyone that may possess unusual or unnatural powers, I believe their thought power can be traced back in time, that they are direct descendants of the Ancients. How many good men have been put to death professing truth, love, happiness . . . persecuted because they knew things other people could not understand. I must say this also about the world today. We are under the influence of those that would rape, pillage, and send this world back to Atlantis. As you know, the Ancients requested their own demise."

"Requested their own destruction?" asked Brunt. "I didn't get this impression when looking at your translations. However, there is much of the material that I don't understand. I can't comprehend what the text refers to when mentioning the dimensions of 1, 2,

3, and 4 as compared to the dimensions of one, two, three and four. Are they not the same – just written differently?"

"When the light is right, you will see, Willie."

"It's beyond me, Eric."

Sheila appeared at the door, "Eric, you must rest. You are pushing yourself too hard."

"I don't have much time, Sheila. It could be anytime now."

Sheila's work with Eric and the study of the materials brought up from below, enabled Sheila to master the thought transference process . . . in accomplishing this, she remembered all the sordid details which occurred to her since her kidnapping. But the interest she had in the subject now at hand superceded her personal feelings over which she now had full control. She realized she was in love with Eric and did not want to leave him, in spite of the tragedy which had occurred.

Eric tossed and turned that night, unable to sleep; something was wrong. Then the same circumstances occurred the following night. Finally on the night of July 16th, he seemed to relax. The following morning he told Sheila, "It happened."

"What has happened?"

"This morning, July 16, 1945, the one thing that had been foretold occurred . . . they split the atom for destruction. We will see the results of this by the pyramid's reaction in a few days; you will see."

Captain Brunt was informed of Eric's vision who then ordered everyone on alert for the next few days . . . for the time Eric feared was coming to pass.

"I don't know how the pyramid will react. How deep can the sub submerge at the point we are now anchored?" Eric asked.

"We are only in 18 feet of water at present. The decks will just be underwater if we submerge in place."

"Good. I believe that will be safe enough."

Captain Brunt wasted no time. He immediately ordered the crew to full alert and instructed the navigator to set the sub on the bottom in the inlet. Eric then requested all to remain quiet so he could feel movement, if there was any; also to keep the periscope up so he could check the outside every half hour. Then Eric requested Johan, Melvin, Peter, Carl and Captain Brunt to meet together and go over everything each one had been doing. Sheila was requested to take notes.

Johan began by reporting the progress on the battery. He stated the pyramid was 16.56 x 16.56 inches at the base, and 15.18 inches on all four slopes, with a height of 11½ inches; the one-third level being 3.67 inches from the base. At that point the carbon from below was placed on each side with the positive and negative poles protruding. The sea water was placed in the cell to a level exactly two-thirds from the peak of the pyramid. "Now all we need is power. I feel Melvin and Peter have a good idea on this. Go ahead Melvin," and Johan relinquished the floor.

Melvin began, "The power source has to do with the pyramid being made of glass. At the one-third level, the sun's rays are directed into the pyramid, on the perpendicular, which I feel increases almost 9 times stronger once inside the pyramid. These rays are then being channeled by the mirrored reflection and are concentrated on one spot. It is like a photocell or tubing with water trapped inside that converts to steam power."

Just then the sub shuddered and moved slightly, as the surrounding area began to shake, as in an earthquake.

"It's started!" Eric shouted as he ran to the periscope. "The water level below must be about to touch the carbon poles. What time is it?"

"0015," came the reply.

"What about our instruments?" Peter asked.

"They're going crazy!" Melvin said, "I have nothing!"

"Keep me posted on any changes, " Eric requested.

"What is happening?" Sheila asked.

"The pyramid below has been disturbed . . . probably a tremor from an earthquake, but it doesn't take much to get it started. In this case the Atom Bomb."

"What will happen, Eric?"

"That's what we're going to find out."

Melvin shouted, "I have a big blip! It's stationary. It just appeared . . . now the blip is getting bigger! Hold it! Another blip! Coming in low from the West. You should see it."

"Yes," Eric said, "I see the landing lights. Quick, Melvin, see if you can identify it!"

Melvin rushed to the periscope and sighted hurriedly. "It's an American PBY seaplane trying to land."

"Very well. Willie, it looks like we may have visitors." Then to Melvin, "What about that larger blip?"

"Sir, it's getting larger. It's surrounding the plane now. I don't see anything but lights. Now they're gone! Where did they go, sir! Look at the screen . . . it's clear!"

"Where could they go? I don't understand. Are you sure the scope is working right, Schmidt?" queried Brunt.

"Yes, sir. And our radio is picking up the plane's home base . . . they are trying to contact them. They are going to search."

"We will have to stay down and hope they don't find us," Captain Brunt said anxiously.

Eric, still somewhat more apprehensive, said, "The cutter will find us but will not report it." Then pacing back and forth, "Damn it! It was too quiet. I expected more!"

Sheila, noting his troubled mind, asked, "Eric, can I help?"

Eric stopped pacing and looked up at Sheila, suddenly realizing his true feelings for her for the first time. The moments their thoughts met, he knew she was in love with him also.

Eric explained, "You realize that although we are in love, we can never be together."

"Yes, I know. But I want to help you to find the answer so you will rest."

"I cannot rest," Eric replied, "I must place the facts in order."

"Maybe I can help. I have gone over the material too. Why not take my thoughts as I saw them?"

"You're right!" exclaimed Eric. "Why didn't I think of that?" It could be so simple that I missed the point. We will get the whole crew to do the same."

Eric called the crew together and explained what he wanted. "Everyone will concentrate on the material that has been gathered. Then at a meeting, I will read everyone's mind to obtain their impressions of the information. Is this agreeable to all?"

All agreed and started to study the sketches, tablets and notes. Meanwhile Oscar planned a new menu to keep the men's morale high during this period and at their peak in order to absorb maximum information.

Three nights later, the sub was brought to deck level. Everyone allowed went on shore to relax. Eric asked if everyone had reviewed and studied all the material . . . but in only three days, not all had the opportunity to scan all the material assembled. It was agreed to hold another meeting in a week which Eric felt would allow enough time for all to finish their tasks.

Sheila stayed close to Eric during the remainder of the week. On the evening of July 29th, she walked up to him and asked, "Do you mind?" Eric stood motionless as Sheila placed a light kiss on his cheek. "I know my reward is being with you."

Eric turned and put his arms around Sheila. He drew her close to him and kissed her tenderly. Still holding Sheila close, Eric said, "You have made everyone's life fuller by staying. During these trying times you have made me happy; happier than I have ever been in my life."

"Thank you, Eric. I love you. Goodnight." Sheila

slipped out of his arms before he could see her tears.

The next morning, the group gathered for their meeting. Eric began immediately, "Okay. Everyone remain quiet and begin to concentrate on the material you have been studying."

All eyes closed as they began to think hard on what they had seen the past week. As Eric passed from one to the other, his eyes began to widen, his breath coming faster. It was as if thirteen computers were channeling all their data into one main unit. The crewmen's minds were data banks sending information to Eric . . . the central processing unit. Suddenly Eric sat down on the floor with his eyes closed, his breathing becoming more labored.

"Stop it! He's exhausted!" cried Sheila. "Stop thinking! Leave!" she implored the men.

All but Brunt left the room. Willie helped Eric to his bed where he fell into a deep sleep. Sheila stayed by him in case he needed attending.

Eric slept for three days. On the 1st of August, he arose refreshed and relaxed, only to find Sheila near exhaustion. He immediately assured her he was fine and told her to go to her quarters and rest. Without much prodding, Sheila went to bed and slept. Her exhausting vigil had completely drained her of strength . . . she also slept for three days.

As Sheila slept, Eric kept busy writing while regaining his strength. Then on the morning of August 5th, Sheila came to Eric. "Eric. Please come!"

"What's up?"

"Just come on!" Sheila replied as she took his hand and led him onto the beach.

"What is it?"

"Just walk. Don't think. Just breathe deeply . . . feel life. Isn't it nice?" Eric smiled and gave no reply . . . just pressed Sheila's hand as they strolled down the beach together.

As they were returning from their walk and within a hundred yards of the sub, Eric suddenly said, "I have that strange feeling again. It's like before . . .

something is wrong. We must hurry. The pyramid is going to act up again." Eric pulled Sheila after him as he raced back to the sub.

Once again inside, Eric called to Brunt, "Willie, we must go on alert again! Something is disturbing the pyramid! You had better order full alert right away!"

"Alright . . . but I have two men on the island. I must get them back here to the sub."

"How long will that take?"

"About thirty minutes."

"Make it less than that, if possible. Speed is essential."

Sheila cornered Willie. "I want to stay on top until we submerge. I hate to be closed up in the sub. I love the fresh air. Let me stay on top until we are ready to go under."

"I suppose that will be alright, but do not leave the ship," Brunt said quickly as he left to summon the men.

Carl was dispatched to get Johan and Peter who he found sun-bathing on the beach. He quickly explained the situation and in fifteen minutes all were aboard . . . but Sheila.

The first shudder came just seconds after the men came aboard. Eric cried out to Willie, "We must go down, now! Submerge! There is no more time!"

"Sheila! Where is Sheila!" cried Brunt.

Carl bounded up the ladder and called to Sheila. She was 200 yards from the sub, standing on the beach, letting the wind blow in her hair and face.

"I can't get her attention, sir!" Carl called to Brunt.

"Come back down!" Brunt commanded. "There is no more time! Take her down! We will hope for the best."

Completely sealed, the sub slipped back into the water. Melvin reported the blip was back on his screen. Eric grabbed the periscope just as the sub rocked from another shudder. He fixed the scope on Sheila as she stood motionless on the beach.

Melvin accentuated his report, "Here it comes! Just as before! It's getting . . . it's here!"

As Eric watched Sheila, he concentrated on her mind. Sheila began to turn, then looked up into the sky. Then as if by a personal touch, Eric felt Sheila's thoughts as she became transparent and vanished. Eric received her thoughts about what she saw, then the fear she felt, as she left. Eric dropped to his knees, exhausted . . . and the crew knew that Sheila was gone.

Just after Sheila disappeared, Melvin announced, "All clear!"

Peter rushed in then and announced, "The radio just announced it! They bombed Hiroshima!"

"Yes," Eric said, "With an Atom Bomb."

Eric had no further words as he went to his cabin. He was exhausted and lay down to sleep again.

"What now, Captain? Do we surface or do we hold?" asked Carl.

"We will sit it out awhile. We dare not move without Eric," said Captain Brunt.

The crew waited patiently, knowing that they were safe for the present. But on the third day, the sub was again rocked by some sort of vibration. Again, Melvin cried, "It's back! The blip is back! It's circling around our location. We seem to be surrounded. Wait! It's gone!"

Peter then said, "The radio reports they have bombed Nagasaki with an Atom Bomb!"

At that moment, Eric appeared and said, "You may surface now. It's all clear."

"Why didn't they take us?" asked Melvin. "We were surrounded."

"I will tell you all in a short time. Please do not press me, as I am almost exhausted again. Where's Oscar?" asked Eric.

"Right here, sir. I have a special meal for you."

"Good. I'm really hungry."

The events of the last few weeks took its toll on the crew. They enjoyed the island . . . but queasily . . . always wondering when and if each moment was going to be their last.

CHAPTER VI

Early the next morning, Johan reported to Eric asking for medical attention. His skin was irritated and red blotches covered his body.

Eric examined him completely and concluded that Johan had radiation poisoning. "Stay out of direct sunlight. Wear a hat, long sleeve shirts, and long pants at all times. That may help."

"Am I going to die from it?"

"I can't tell yet, Johan. Just be sure to avoid direct sunlight and apply this ointment four times a day."

That evening, the American PT Boat returned. Eric requested that its captain be brought aboard. Carl escorted the captain to Eric's stateroom. Mentally, Eric suggested to the captain that he return to the sub with enough official papers, forms, stamps and seals along with an American typewriter so that fictitious papers could be initiated for the submarine crew. "I will also need twelve American names and biographies for my people. You will return in a week with enough supplies for twelve sets of identity papers. Now go."

Later, Captain Brunt confronted Eric. "What are you up to Eric? You have been real nervous lately."

"I know, Willie. I grew fond of having Sheila around and now I feel a little empty at times."

"I can sympathize with you on that. We all miss her. But we must get out of this situation or we are all doomed."

"Don't worry, Willie. The American PT Boat captain will return with your freedom. You'll see. We must call the men together tomorrow morning. I will explain the plan I have formulated and then start preparations for implementing it."

After breakfast the next day, everyone was assembled under the pines which bowed in the constant breeze. The time spent on the island had been magnificent and Eric regretted he and the men would have to end their sojourn. He addressed the men, "First, all of you will know of the power of the Ancients, as I call them. It will endow you with power for the present and certain powers for your future. You will remember it as a dream, yet when you leave this island, it will be as if you had always known this power."

Everyone looked at each other in puzzlement.

Eric continued, "When the American captain returns, five men will return with the PT Boat to a point near its base and from there it will be up to you to get to America and start life anew as Americans. I have no doubt that you will make it — just remember you have the power to suggest your will on others. You will remember your stay here only as a dream. Now I am going to start at the beginning and go straight through to the present."

"Wait a minute! What about the rest of us? Why only five?" Carl asked.

Eric responded, "Oh, yes. As the boat returns each time, five more will go until everyone has left and hopefully relocated in America. Any more questions for now?"

Hearing none, Eric continued, "Do all of you understand evolution as it occurred over the years? If not, picture an apeman crawling along through life when a super-intelligent being landed on Earth, arriving in a unit say . . . like our submarine . . . the main difference being that unit could travel from star to star.

"These beings lived a long time because, in travel, they slept and were dormant, thus conserving their energy. I first thought the crying face in the pyramid below was placed there as a tribute to a dying planet in another galaxy, but I realize now that it relates to our planet. These travelers from time or space were called sons of God; they were able to create landing fields and a guiding beacon — the beacon being the pyramid — for their craft. They used the pyramid as a beacon with the glow given off by the pyramid caused by ultraviolet rays from the sun. From the dark side of the Earth, this glow appeared as a white dot in the darkness. Thus, they could navigate and negotiate landings. Once landed, they walked among the apemen and with their thought transference ability, controlled every move they made.

"As time passed, the aliens were successful in penetrating the deepest mind recesses of the ape beings of this planet. They were able to implant suggestions for the humanization of certain species and, in doing so, caused their downfall. Initially, it was not their intent to mate with these female creatures, but as time passed, they succumbed to their temptations. In time, the combination of woman mating with the intelligent beings produced such a disaster that even He sorrowed over the creation of man and prepared to destroy all mankind — but relented at the last moment and saved one called Noah. The area of Atlantis was destroyed by the rising waters from the continual rains. Only Noah survived. The covenant of light, which we know as the rainbow, was left to show that the Earth would not be destroyed by flood again. But through the ages, man again failed. Sodom and Gommorah came next. He was so displeased with what he saw, he caused them to be blasted away. But prior to the blast people were punished, if you will remember, by being cast blind through sheer suggestion. To carry this further, Lot's daughter lay with him to conceive and carry on the bloodlines. One offspring resulted . . . Joseph. But when he died, so did the intelligence. Not until Moses did it return.

"Now I ask you, can you be at peace with others as well as yourself? By this I mean, harboring no thoughts of wanting material things or desiring more than you have; no anger within your soul, just a peaceful feeling within you. It is necessary to be at peace before you can exercise the power; you must seek love and be completely at rest. Then the intelligence comes to you. Some men clamor to see God, to speak to

Him, to know Him. But I tell you God is love, the energy is light. Be at peace and you will know this.

"When the great flood destroyed Atlantis, the pyramid was trapped by the waters. Because it is still wet, it maintains its power source and continues to function. The pyramids in Egypt, however, are dry thus they are not fully active. The sun's ultraviolet rays cause anything placed in the chamber to remain unchanged, or as the Ancients called it, immortal. That is, any object placed in the room never dulls, never rusts, instead becomes perpetual. In the future, operational units will be built like this with material that will be everlasting and the operation continuous and with very little maintenance required.

"Now I come to power. The power is thought, whether you think, he thinks, or she thinks. If you possess the power, you will be mocked, taunted, even ridiculed. But the compensations are infinitely great. The power allows you to feel no pain, to heal yourself and others. It will even allow you to move objects, or yourself, or others. To utilize this power you must first place yourself at rest and relax completely, concentrate on relaxing. You have no wants, you feel good. The more you relax, the more you wish to sleep. You feel warm and comfortable, your eyes wish to close. You wish to see the sun, you relax even deeper. At this point of relaxation, if you wish to maintain this feeling, all you have to say is 'ALPHA' and you will be in a relaxed state. Anytime you wish to relax again, say 'ALPHA' and it will occur. Now each of you say 'ALPHA' . . .

"If you are who you are, know that you are who you are, the following is possible. Remember, if you are requesting pain to stop, or to numb your teeth, or for bleeding to stop, then do the following. Say aloud, 'My name is . . . , I am sure I know this to be a fact.' Then say, 'It doesn't hurt, it will not bleed, and there will be no after-effects.' Again, if you are who you say you are, the above is fact. I must emphasize that this is no game and you must be in pain, or bleeding, and in need of healing. Again, I challenge you, if you are who you say you are, then heal it. Conquer this and you may proceed to other challenges. Studies can be made easier by saying aloud, 'I will retain all I read.' Once again, are you sure you are who you say you are?

"Once your power is increased, you will be able to accomplish levitation, but for this you must be strong because the drain on the mind is excessive. Begin again by relaxing and concentrating. Say 'ALPHA' followed by 'BEND' and move the item you wish. You must have your mind 'UP' and concentrating deeply. When completed, again say 'OMEGA'. This effort will make you feel very weary — drained of all energy — and you must sleep to replenish your energy level. As you know, I sleep for three entire days.

"In order to move from one place to another, you must be at peace and again fully relaxed. Say 'ALPHA' then picture yourself at the place where you want to be and say, 'NO WHEN'. Here again, the brain must be at full strength. I am still working on the development of this activity, but I know that as you go from one dimension to another, without 'WHEN' you leave the fourth and travel in the second or third dimension. Again, remember to say 'OMEGA' when finished.

"The first dimension is the ruler of the Universe. In the tablet's words, the first of the second, third and fourth. You must think as the first — be at peace, love mankind, harbor no wants or desires, for without the first, 'ALPHA' has no meaning or power, nor has 'OMEGA'. Without it, you could never possess the power.

"It was written by the Ancients that 'The Spirit was removed from man.' You must return to and be part of the Spirit. Then you can do the things I spoke of. Now I am going to mentally suggest to you that this is but a dream. In your new life, in your new world, if you continue to have wants and desires, you will forfeit the power, you will not be of the Spirit. I have given you the full meaning of the tablets and notes, as I now understand them.

"Now I will tell you about Sheila. By thought process, I had asked Sheila to depart from us to try and learn more. To please me she agreed."

"Where did she go, Eric?" queried Captain Brunt.

"She tried to give me a mental picture, but all I could see was a sphere. But one thing I do know, while I slept, her thoughts came to me and told me to stand on that same spot on December 5th."

"This year?" Carl asked.

"Yes," replied Eric, and continued, "the PT Boat captain will return in a few nights. I want the following men ready to leave with it: Paul Durbin, Peter Loften, Herman Kofcher, Paul Rumal and Verne Hagen. Now let's break this up and everyone get back to enjoying these last few days here on our paradise island."

CHAPTER VII

The dark starless night provided deep cover for the PT Boat as she came alongside the U-237 submarine. Eric greeted the PT Boat captain with a cordial, "Good evening. I see you accomplished your task. Good work. Please instruct your men to stand by. Your return trip should begin within the hour."

Minutes later, Eric was making his way to his small shack he had established as his island headquarters. He knew that in a little while there would be five less Germans in the world and five additional Americans.

After an hour of concentrated effort, study and typing, Eric finished the identities and biographies of the American names assigned to the first five to leave. The life history accompanying each provided a variety of backgrounds that Eric knew could be matched to each sub crewman. A background best suited to the man's natural aptitudes.

Eric arose from his paper-strewn desk and rang a bell. Immediately Oscar Hiney appeared, "Yes sir, can I help you?"

"Please locate Paul Durbin, Peter Loften, Paul Rumal, Herman Kofcher and Verne Hagen. Send each one to see me, one at a time, beginning with Peter. I'll need five minutes with each man, Oscar, so allow that much of an interval before sending the next man in to see me. And also, make sure Verne is the last man sent in to me. Now go find these five while I get ready. Thank you."

As Oscar went in search of the men, Eric laid down on his back on a seven foot wooden plank placed in a North-South direction. He closed his eyes and concentrated deeply. The plank was suspended from the ceiling by two strong ropes tied to each end of the board. This rigid hammock-like structure had served as Eric's bed for the past few weeks and now served him as a meditation board.

Exactly five minutes had passed when Oscar announced that the five men were assembled and ready. Eric addressed them as a group, "You have been loyal sailors and I personally want to commend you for your spirit in the face of adversity. Through the transference process which we talked about, it is now possible for you to have a chance for a new life. You are all good men and will continue to be so, but it will be as Americans that you must begin anew."

"Will we completely lose our old identity?" asked Peter Loften.

"No. All you will lose is your name and the remembrance of all this. Let us begin . . . I will now see each one of you men separately for a few minutes. Then you will board the PT Boat as American men with American names. At some future date you will have a strong dream which will recall you to Germany. I can't say just how long a time this will be until it can be accomplished. I expect it depends on the path mankind chooses to follow. For now, all you need to know is that you're being given a chance to be reborn into a new life. See what good you can accomplish!"

Peter entered the shack with Eric. Once inside, Eric looked deep and penetrating into Peter's eyes. With his thought transference he was able to change this 22 year old German into a top-notch mechanic by the name of Jack Chandler, age 23, with good mechanical ability. "You will find employment near the ocean where you can pursue your hobby of deep sea diving." Once completed, Eric bade 'goodbye' to one Jack Chandler.

In the same manner he transformed Paul Durbin, diver and mechanic, into George Gonyu, age 22 recently discharged from the U.S. Navy and ready to start college. Similarly Paul Rumal another instrument man on the U-237, became Ralph Smith, age 22, with training in instrumentation and the ability to formulate new designs for precise medical tools.

Herman Kofcher, torpedo man, formerly a welder, was now a welder again with the name of William Harris, age 24.

Finally, it was time for Eric to interview Verne Hagen. Verne had been the pump operator aboard the sub and Eric had noticed a lack of learning ability inherent in his make-up. He therefore assigned Hagen the identity of a sports-loving outdoorsman, a good hunter and fisherman who could provide for himself in the forests of America. In this way, Eric hoped to forestall tragedy for Verne . . . in case the thought transference process reversed itself and left him in a bewildered state of mind. With a fairly low intelligence level, Eric was not sure how deep his thought transference would root, therefore the outdoors would be safer for Verne in case of reversion. At least he could start him in his new life as Bill Johnson, and continue to hope the thought transfer would hold.

The five men now aboard the boat received a last thought from Eric reinforcing the idea that their life since the U-237 had disengaged itself from the war, was only a dream. Just prior to the boat departing Eric again implanted the suggestion for the boat to return in two weeks.

Eric watched the boat depart with part of the crew and wished them luck. Then he immediately gathered the remaining seven and explained the order of departure. "The next five men to go will be, Captain Willie Brunt, Carl Schultz, Melvin Schmidt, Oscar Hiney and Heinrich Goulstadt."

No one opposed Eric's directives, for by this time, they all had turned the decision-making over to him and acknowledged him as leader. They began discussing what the future would hold for them. Eric and the men began an earnest discussion of the current situation and what a depressing time it was for the people now living.

Eric voiced his opinion that the world could be a better place to live than it was now and it was up to them to try and help. He explained, "As you go through your new life, with a new name and identity, you will not lose your soul. The thought process that I instill in you will continue to grow stronger as you tread life's path. However, until it is time for you to leave here, I suggest we just enjoy the leisure time we have remaining and not concern ourselves with the future. The future will be here soon enough." Eric returned to his shack to complete the remaining seven identities.

The two weeks slipped by so fast that it was hard for them to believe it was now September 2, 1945, and the PT Boat would soon be arriving.

Then as it came into view and finally pulled alongside the U-237, the men who were to leave on this run were instructed to report to Eric in his shack.

Eric embraced Willie Brunt and assured him his new life would go smoothly. He then transferred the character of Captain H.R. Sawyer to Brunt, and through this thought transference process, Brunt became a 37 year old pleasure boat captain. As a part of his crew, Melvin Schmidt became Donald Wilson, age 24, assigned the duty as radioman.

Eric then grasped Carl Schultz's hand and looked steadily into his eyes. Carl became James MacDonald, age 20, ready to enroll in college to major in electronics.

Heinrich Goulstadt was transformed into the identity of John Richardson, age 24, painter and sculptor, destined for great fame.

Finally, Eric embraced Oscar Hiney and told him, "Your ingenuity aboard the U-237 in the preparation of meals will not go unrewarded. In your new life, you will be recognized as the true creative genius you are. You will be S. Thomas Henry, and become a Master Chef of wide reputation."

He then recycled the thought process, suggesting again to all, that this will be remembered only as a dream. Wishing them all the best of luck, he reminded them that he would be in contact with them at a later time and they would see each other again.

When the boat pulled out, its load of supplies

replaced by human cargo, Carl remarked to Eric, "It's sad to see us split up."

"I know, Carl, but we must go on. There are things in life that we must accomplish, and we can't do them in our present situation."

Johan then asked, "What about us three? Can you tell us now what is in store for us?"

"Did you notice that I suggested that the boat return on December 6th? That is three months from now and we will need all that time to finish our mission here. You, Carl Hinze, and I will be quite busy right up to that time."

"What do we have to do?"

"We must put the sub back in the pyramid along with the tablet. For that reason, we must begin work at once to make the sub operational with a crew of only three men. We must utilize every trick we can think of to make its operation as automatic as possible . . . so we can act as monitors to insure the proper functioning of the entire submarine."

"Are you serious, Eric? Three men to run a sub by themselves?" John said unbelievingly.

"Are we really going to put the tablet back in the pyramid?" queried Carl.

"Yes, and I believe we must do it by the middle of November. I can't say any more now. It must be done."

So each dawn brought new inventions and theories to try and steadily they rigged the controls so that it was possible to operate the sub with a crew of three. When they had finished all they could possibly do, Johan suggested a trial run.

"There is no time for that," Eric replied. "We must start at once! Johan, you have continued to put your best effort into this work, and I saw day by day that your pain increased from the burns you possess. Your condition is critical now, as I think you have guessed. However, the spirit in which you continued your work proves to me that you must be one of the chosen. I believe you will be cured when we get to the pyramid."

"Have you known about my condition all along?" asked Johan.

"Some time ago I suspected it. As for your being healed, from my most recent studies and the thoughts I have received, it seems virtually sure that you will be well again."

"Eric, I hope you are right."

"Also Johan and Carl, today is November 20th, and the vibrations I have been receiving are very strong, urging me to start our journey immediately. If we cannot go today, I fear we won't have time to complete our trip and be back here when the boat returns. Therefore, we must leave today." With this said, Eric left for his shack to gather the tablets for the trip to the pyramid.

"Only two diving units work, Carl," reminded Johan.

"You're right! Let's go by ourselves. Eric need not know." Then, thoughtfully, Carl added, "We will leave the supplies on the landing and go aboard . . . and Johan, watch your thoughts, if Eric reads our minds, we will never make it."

"Then hurry, Carl! Eric is up at the town. If we go now, we can make it!"

In fifteen minutes Carl was pulling in the last hatch and sealing the U-237 for its last dive. Just as Carl and Johan began backing the sub, Eric realized what they were doing. But it was too late to catch them as the sub submerged.

Eric tried to follow their thoughts, but he could not reach them by suggestion through the water and rocks below. He began to pace back and forth, then finally retired to the shacks which had been built by the men.

Carl and Johan had their hands full trying to guide the sub to the location where they had previously encountered the channel opening. When Johan announced they were there, Carl stopped all engines and began to take on ballast to submerge to 184 feet below the surface. They realized the extra work required with two men instead of three and with relentless pursuit and boundless energy managed to navigate the opening and grinding passage through to the chamber. Finally, the sub bobbed up and rested with a slight rocking motion.

"This must be it! My gauge indicates surface level!"

Carl put the periscope up. "The greenish light! We're here again! C'mon, let's go!"

"Carl, I'll never make it. I feel too weak."

"Sure you will! Here, I'll give you a hand getting into your diving suit."

Once dressed in the diving outfits, Carl cracked the hatch and again smelled the old musty odor. "C'mon on, Johan, I'll give you a hand out."

Both men were standing on the chamber's marble entrance slab and could see their fallen comrades lying just where they had been left with absolutely no change in their appearance.

"Okay, in you go Johan," said Carl as he gave him a shove into the water . . . then jumped in behind him. As they went under the rock, Johan kept falling back. Carl grabbed him and began working his way out. Just as he reached the clearing, Carl lost his grip on Johan. The current caught Johan and swept him back into the pyramid. Carl realized the current was pulling so hard that he could not go back for Johan. He would need every bit of his energy to keep going and make steady progress. Finally, he got clear and began his slow ascent to the top. He knew he had to stay below his air bubbles or he would get the bends. Exhausted and weak from the struggle, Carl reached the surface, swam to the beach and blacked out. He had used every ounce of strength he had.

Johan, meanwhile, maneuvered himself to the sub where he entered and fell onto the floor, realizing this was the end. But by reaching the sub, had maintained in a sense, immortality. He too would be a mummy.

When Carl regained consciousness, Eric was standing over him. He had been stripped of his diving equipment for many days had passed. They didn't speak of Johan, as both men knew he was lost to them forever. Eric saw how upset Carl was by the loss of his friend and his failure to save him . . . so he immediately blanked the incident from Carl's mind.

"Come," said Eric, "We must bury all these items."

Later, Carl and Eric sat at the shack on the island. Carl asked, "What's to become of me?"

Eric responded, "From this time forward, each year that you now live, will be but a half-year. You will continue to be an engineer, although you will now continue life in America as the others. Your name will be Sam Jones. All this will be a dream until later on. In time you will remember. Tomorrow is December 5th. When the ground shudders, you must get in the old pirate's well and stay there for a count of 50. When you crawl out, you will be okay until the PT Boat comes. Then you will live life anew."

Early the next morning, Eric was on the spot where Sheila had last stood. All day he waited but nothing happened. Then at 1722 hours, Eric heard planes and the earth began to shudder. Within the next five minutes, five TBM bombers were over him but within seconds . . . disappeared, yet Eric remained in his original spot. Carl came out of the well and Eric shouted, "Go back! It's not over! They will try again!"

Again Eric stood patiently . . . then another tremor shook the earth again, and this time Eric disappeared along with a lone PBY bomber on the southern horizon.

Eric was aware of every molecule in his body. It felt like they were all separating, yet he felt no pain. In the next moment he re-materialized in a hooded capsule that was glassed in. Next to him was Sheila, fast asleep, with a small tube in her mouth. She was still beautiful to Eric.

A voice questioned Eric, "Are you a son of Dirt or are you a son of God?"

Eric answered, "I am made of dirt, but I am at peace. I am a man of God." Eric now realized that the chamber in the pyramid was the transformation room the travelers used to make their transitions to earth. He knew he was in the chamber now for the transition from man to spirit. He could not help wondering why he had been chosen.

"Were you not raised in evil to find peace, and master the power of thought? Therefore, you may travel with us. Man has devised his own destruction of hellfires and brimstone. We are not needed here."

Eric then received a thought for him to take the pill located on a shelf over his head and to insert the tube protruding from the side of the capsule into his mouth. This was the last thing he would remember for many Earth years.

The following day, December 6th, 1945, the PT Boat returned to the island to find only Carl Hinze there. Carl boarded the boat and returned to start anew in America as Sam Jones. In years to come, odd thoughts would cross his mind from time to time but always they would lurk just below his level of consciousness. Only vaguely would he remember a recurring dream he had of life in a German submarine. Most of his thoughts would be concentrated on further developing his engineering and political careers. He would successfully structure a top-notch group of men into a very successful and profitable engineering firm.

Having time and money to spare, he would enter politics and concern himself with gaining more power and prestige. He would become devoted to the acquisition of more material things . . . more money . . . more power. There was no time to worry about this dream which kept nagging at him. Dream theory or self-analysis? No time! Sam Jones was to be a busy man for quite some time to come.

CHAPTER VIII

On March 15, 1974, Doctor Eric von Wilhelm awoke from a dream to find himself enclosed in a clear glass capsule. "Where am I?" he questioned as he turned his head to survey his surroundings. The light surrounding him was so bright he could hardly see, yet there was no pain in his eyes from the glare. "Am I late? I must have overslept. Is the crew already up?"

Gradually, Eric realized he was not in the submarine. These surroundings were not familiar to him at all. Then, as his thoughts grew clearer and he recalled more, it was as if he were walking through a deep fog very slowly, making it possible to see more clearly with each step. Then like dawn breaking, he remembered everything.

I left Earth on December 5th, 1945. I left behind war, poverty and despair. There was a storm and I escaped. I came here and found Sheila encapsulated with a tube in her mouth. I remember taking a pill and putting a tube in my own mouth. How long ago did I take the pill?

Eric took the tube from his mouth and examined his hands. They had not aged. He was the same. He looked over to where Sheila had lain, but her capsule was empty. Eric became concerned and was ready to call out for Sheila, when a voice came to him.

"It is now March 15, 1974, Earth time. Do you wish to get up, Eric von Wilhelm?"

"Yes," replied Eric. "Where's Sheila?"

"She is here. If you wish to get up, all you have to do is think about it."

Eric began to rise but then hesitated. "What about this capsule? I can't find any opening." As he spoke the door opened automatically and Eric stepped out.

"You need exert no physical force to open doors

now. All you need do is to think where you wish to be and it will be so."

"Who are you?" Eric questioned looking for the source of the voice.

"I am spirit just as you are now. If you wish me to appear as you would want me to look, I will appear in that form."

"What are you saying?" Eric thought.

"You have gone through the 28 years passage to remove the flesh and arrive in the Spirit. You can see, feel, and talk by your own thoughts. Some of the answers you already know, if you will think about it," replied the voice.

"Yes. I see now that a kind of voyage is required to pass from flesh to spirit. Now that we are away from the planet Earth, I feel relaxed and at peace."

"Yes," came the reply. "Now that man has devised his own method of destruction with the Atom Bomb, we are no longer needed by them. For centuries we of the 2nd Dimension have stayed here in orbit trying to maintain a balance on Earth. Our vigil was one of peace. We have existed alongside Earth trying to protect matter and anti-matter. Just as you see the stars, sun, and the visible light, it is as a dream. The light actually occurred before you lived, as far as that goes, before anyone lived. The life on Earth is in the past tense. When the Spirit was removed, the life of the flesh has always been talked about in the past tense. The only future to earthlings is the Spirit. Look at any subject, its outcome or answer is already known. The true future is in the Spirit. My light is the black light, which is my energy . . . and now yours. To possess the power of the black light is to possess the true perpetual Spirit World."

For a fleeting moment Eric thought of the submarine crew and Earth as he had known it.

"Do you wish to travel with us now?" queried the voice.

"Us?" Then Eric realized he had not looked for Sheila. "Where is Sheila? Is she alright?"

"I am here, Eric. I have been watching you for

months. When my time passage was up, I arose and have been watching you ever since. Oh Eric, how I have missed you."

Eric turned and saw Sheila. How beautiful she looked. He reached out as to touch her hand, and it was as if they had touched for they felt a communion between them that no one of the flesh ever experienced. An overflowing of love and peace consumed them.

"Again I ask you. Do you wish to travel with us? Most earthlings desire the flesh and its offerings, yet does a man finally retire from earth by dying? Does the mind not come to full rest? It is at this time that thought places them in the position so desired. In so many cases their wish is of Earth . . . that is why they are still there. As like them, you also have a choice."

"I do not wish to stay on Earth," Eric thought.

"You may return to Earth only once and stay only 24 hours; if you do not wish yourself back here, you will remain forever on Earth."

"Yes," replied Eric, "we are bound in the Spirit."

"So be it." came the voice. "Plan your trip now. We will leave for Earth in a little while."

Sheila did not want to be without Eric again. "I'll follow you wherever you go."

"The only person I wish to see now is Sam Jones, as he is known in America. The others seem to be doing well in their situations and are controlling their powers well."

With that thought in mind, Eric and Sheila found themselves standing next to Carl who was busy seeing another customer in his office. Carl had already amassed a fortune but wanted more. His greed for more money and more material things was hidden behind the veneer of the typical businessman; regularly attending church, donating large sums of money to various charitable organizations, a local politician, chamber of commerce president and Little League sponsor. Underneath this cloak of respectability resided a vicious spirit ready to backstab another man if it would advance his own personal position or wealth.

When Sam Jones finished his conversation with his customer, Eric gave the suggestion that when he turned he would be able to see Sheila and him as he remembered them. In appearance, Carl had only changed slightly since he was aging only half a year for each calendar year he lived. Instead of being fifty-six he was now only forty-two.

As Carl turned, he gasped, then said, "Excuse me, you two remind me of someone I know, I mean knew. What can I do for you?"

Eric spoke, "Do you not know us?"

"I feel as if I do . . . but I meet so many people in my business. I can't remember everyone. What's on your mind . . . and please be brief, I've got to go to a meeting in a few minutes."

Eric realized that Carl had really taken Sam Jones' identity to heart, and that he would have to proceed slowly with him. "Carl, don't you remember us? Eric and Sheila?"

Carl began to get dizzy and slowly sat down. "That was all a dream. It wasn't real!" and began to rub his forehead with both hands.

"Don't you remember the island and the sub? Also the pyramid? Do you remember when you left to come to America by way of the PT Boat?"

"Yes!" Carl shouted, "But I can't believe it was real! I refuse . . . "

Eric interrupted, "I see you use the power in business and politics to your advantage. Because of the power you have been very successful in acquiring wealth. But what good have you accomplished with it? I have spent the last twenty-eight years removing the flesh and obtaining the Spirit. You have used the power of thought for your own material and worldly gains. Don't you realize the world must change to be saved from total annihilation?"

Carl buzzed his secretary and told her to cancel the scheduled meeting and to allow for no interruptions. "I know now that my present life is the one that is a dream."

"That is true," Eric said. "You will live the rest of your life with full knowledge of your previous existence."

"How has all this happened? I cannot comprehend how one person can be two? What is the secret? Does the Spirit enable this to occur? What of God?" Carl asked.

"Even I have not seen God, but I know of Him, as you can and possibly will."

"How will I explain such a change of personality and lifestyle to other people? They will think I've lost my mind and gone crazy!"

"Have you forgotten your ability to suggest? People will accept the change because you will suggest acceptance to them. Just as we have suggested that you see us, so you can do the same."

"What do I do?"

"First, you must sit down and write all you know and all you have been told so the world will know," said Sheila.

"I cannot write or spell well, Sheila."

"It doesn't matter. Your thoughts will be transmitted into the proper words; you'll see."

"It is important to emphasize that a person must be at peace with himself and others. Then he will not want, and it will be possible to possess the power," said Eric.

"What of those who will not heed my suggestion?" Carl asked.

"There are those who will not heed nor understand. They are led into their follies. Those of middle-range intelligence are also led by the thought process to form concepts of right or wrong. You have seen the results since you have been using the power in politics. Lust, greed, hate – they must be stamped out on all levels! If only twenty percent of the population is consumed with this worldly philosophy, it will cause the destruction of the planet Earth."

"Right now," Sheila continued, "countries are in

turmoil because of desires. The people of the world are in the Garden of Eden, but without the Spirit. They only need to be at peace, free from their desires, and the warmth of the Spirit will flow through them and remove pain, hunger, and cold. God removed the Spirit from man because it was being misused. But all the flesh has to do is accept the spirit that exists in peace and love and the Garden of Eden will bloom again. Remember all these things when you write."

Eric said, "I now suggest to you that you will remember all I and Sheila have told you . . . but you will not remember seeing either of us. We must go now, as we have used all of our alloted time." With these words, Sheila and Eric disappeared.

Carl immediately began to write. "At 2000 hours, on the evening of April 13, 1945 . . . " stopping, he said to himself. "I'll tell someone. They must understand!"

Sheila and Eric returned to the Second Dimension of the Black Light and informed the voice, "We are ready now."

"Good," said the voice, "we will travel to a planet in the Third Galaxy which has its own time. Do not think back to Earth, for as you know, thought is all you need to place you there. Now think of 'SPECTRA', the fourth planet in the Third Galaxy and we will be there."

In a moment they were over the planet 'SPECTRA', looking down on an area known as the "TRIANGLE OF THE HEAVENS". The voice spoke. "This will be your final test. As you have heard of purgatory before Heaven, this will be your preparation for infinity and your place in the Second Dimension of the Black Light . . . now prepare to make your transition."

CHAPTER IX

Making the spiritual transition to the planet would require little effort. It was just a matter of placing themselves through thought transference, into the accepted shuttle craft of the planet Spectra and landing.

The Voice spoke. "There are things you must know before you transit. As you will find out, Spectra is three hundred years ahead of Earth. The inhabitants are, as you were, of flesh and their society quite complex in that everything is controlled by computer. These computers run on energy cells that have a half-life of 25,000 years. Two hundred and fifty years ago, a known scientist set up these computers programming everything concerning the inhabitants' traits into them. They were fed an individual's birth, eventual IQ, abilities, and from this information, placed him in his or her work.

"As for sickness, the computers were programmed for medicine and death. At no point were the computers programmed for God, thus no mention of faith as of now has been made. The reason for this is readily seen. Through the continual use of dope and drugs by past generations, all offspring are now addicts. Gradually the old died out, leaving addicts at the mercy of the computers, which now punish the young inhabitants by cutting off their drugs, causing severe withdrawals and even deaths.

"The offspring know nothing of how the computers work, only that they live by them. The High Priest, or main computer operator, key-punches newborns and from then on the computers do the rest — even to holding court trials. Yet, the so-called criminals of the planet will be your best contact, even though they do not understand. Also, some of the older prisoners have dried out and are able to work the fields — and have even developed common sense.

They expect a prophet or wise one to come and lead them.

"Now, in a few moments a couple will crash in their craft, killing them, and the sensors of the computers will pick up their deaths unless you act fast. No other thoughts now, GO! You know what you must do. I will be here two years from now."

Without further hesitation, Eric and Sheila found themselves in the Spectra couple's forms skimming along a smooth surface in a round and tubular unit propelled by an electro-magnetic force. Longer units were cutting through the fields thus producing the energy for the smaller units. Glancing around, Eric spotted a small electric burner with incense and marijuana smoking away.

Sheila spoke. "Where are we headed for, Eric?"

"I don't know Sheila, but you must remember we are programmed for somewhere. First thing I better do, is put out this smoking unit or we will be one of them sooner than we anticipate. If you can recall drugs are not effective on flesh . . . only the mind. So we must watch ourselves . . . as we are programmed to completely act of the flesh."

There were two earphones in the unit, each containing a musical note appealing to the recent inhabitants, now removed. As Eric listened, he spoke to Sheila. "This could really scramble your head, a constant note like this."

Sheila frowned and said, "I can't take it."

About this time, the unit moved off the main fairway into a settlement of homes at different elevations. No one housing unit was level with another. Then, without notice, the capsule stopped within a closed room. By stepping out and to the left, into an elevator, Eric and Sheila were carried to their new home two stories off the ground.

As the door opened, the view which greeted them was amazing. It was arranged so that even an amputee could get to any place in the apartment without any trouble. The ceiling contained ultraviolet lamps, three walls had moving scenes of the planet

Spectra, while on the back wall a screen and selector panel was mounted for viewing, phoning and reporting. In the corner, another electric burner filled with marijuana was smoking. Eric quickly placed the lid over it.

Sheila, meantime, pressed the snack button and a tray appeared with a glass of milk and a piece of pie. But before Sheila could touch it, Eric put his finger in the milk and tasted it.

"Just as I thought," Eric said, "Laced with cocaine. Probably in the pie also. We will have to watch what we eat and drink. We will boil water and let it cool for drinking."

"If this be the case here, what about the main buildings and cafeterias? It will be the same. Also, what about the air? It's filled with this smoke."

Eric was deep in thought as he answered. "Forget about that for now. We will be tested soon by the computers. We must act like we have had too much drugs, so we will be restricted from exposure. Also, we know from the thoughts of the other couple, we will be joined by a group of Spectrans for our weekly get-together and games. We better, no wait . . . a special newscast is coming on the screen."

Over the screen appeared the trial of a young girl, not even fourteen, who, without remembering, had arose late one night at her home, where a get-together was in progress, and had joined in and copulated with all the males present as her mother had. She had become pregnant from this orgy which upset the computers who were in charge of keeping the population in line and designating those eligible for children — all others being sterilized at age sixteen. To go against the computers was considered a crime and punishable by death, since having offspring caused drug dosages to be reduced in the girl to insure the offspring's survival and non-malformation. Since the girl had been exposed to a continual excessive amount of drugs, both her and her unborn child would live no more. Her sentence was no drugs for one month, then extermination . . . providing she was not already dead. The mother was given a sentence of one month without drugs for not administering the birth control pill to her daughter. The same term was given to the father for having sexual relations with his daughter. All others involved were released.

Sheila gasped. "These people act like dogs! Although not made like dogs, they remain in heat one hundred percent of the time, and with the sterilization process, don't hesitate to copulate or fornicate!"

"I know," replied Eric, "and tonight we will be joined by just such a group. So try and read out their thoughts . . . what they expect of you. Give them the thought you want them to have. Remember, we must get through these first few days in the hope of reaching someone."

Eric placed some wood chips from the furniture in the incense burner to have the air smoky and sweet-smelling, while Sheila prepared some carrots and celery, by juicing them, for her and Eric.

Later, as the guests began to arrive, Eric became alarmed . . . for as he greeted each one, he realized they had no thoughts, only drives. As the evening wore on, the ear-splitting whine of the individual notes emanating from the group, now all mixed together, plus the swaying of the guests, began to disgust Eric. He stood over one young man sitting with his legs crossed and swaying with his eyes closed. Eric immediately tried to impress his thoughts on him, but not to Eric's surprise, there was no response.

Sheila immediately felt the dismay Eric experienced. They both knew they were in trouble. Eric looked over at Sheila and realized she was scared and somehow felt her thoughts might turn back to the night on the island when she was raped.

Eric immediately gave her the thought, "If you are grabbed for sex, it will be as if it were me." Sheila nodded her understanding.

Then the orgy began. Everyone participated as a group at first, then they split up in pairs. Eric saw his chance and grabbed Sheila and held her close.

Suddenly to Eric's surprise, the front door burst

open and computer guards rushed in and began to pull the couples apart and carrying them out. Eric told Sheila, "Relax. Act drugged so the guards will take us also."

Downstairs, a large unit was waiting to transport them to computer headquarters. Upon arriving, blood samples were taken by eunuch-like attendants and then Eric and Sheila were shuttled into a room.

The eunuchs were bred by women raised in captivity without drugs. Then these men, their off-springs, were castrated and later trained as guards, attendants, doctors, and the many other necessary trades and professions on Spectra.

While waiting, Eric mentally told Sheila. "This is madness! Naziism! Dope! Only machines could do this! There's no thought in any of these Spectrans!"

The door opened and one large eunuch entered. "All others have been released. You two must come with me."

Eric and Sheila followed the eunuch down a long corridor where electric eyes and lasers were installed at and over each door leading into it. It was obvious that once confined, occupants could not escape. At the end of the corridor was a room marked EXAM. This turned out to be their destination.

Once in the room, they noticed the main computer desk . . . clean except for keys used in punching cards. Sitting there was an elderly eunuch who seemed drowsy from being awakened.

He began to question Eric and Sheila as to why their blood samples showed a reduced trace of drugs for it was law that all inhabitants would ingest a prescribed drug dosage.

Eric felt there was a chance of them being tried and both he and Sheila sent to a farm. This would enable him to get in contact with those who would be open to suggestions — that is, if this eunuch would take his suggestions.

Eric began to use his thought transference and at first the elder eunuch did not respond, but kept saying, "Need to send for more drugs." Then it took. "Okay.

You two have broken the law. So the great computer will decide." As he pushed the keys, Eric hoped he had also reached him for the proper key-punching.

The eunuch pushed one final button and another guard entered. "Take them to trial before the great computer," he said and departed through another door.

With that, they left the room to be taken to the computerized Magistrate. On board the conveyor, Eric mentally told Sheila not to worry. "I think I reached him before he pushed the wrong keys."

"I feel you did, too," Sheila said.

The unit stopped outside a large building. As they were led into the great room, echoes of their footsteps could be heard. Towards the rear of the large room was a prisoner box in which they were placed. On the wall facing them was a large screen. To the right of the screen was a computer marked JURY and to the left of this picture screen, a computer marked JUDGE.

A picture appeared on the screen of Eric and Sheila showing their actions leading to the incident of their arrest, with sections left out which Eric knew was the result of his suggestion to the elderly eunuch. When the pictures were finished, the whirring computers of the JURY were heard, followed by the one marked JUDGE. Finally, a computerized voice stated, "YOU ARE HEREBY JUDGED INSANE AND ARE COMMITTED TO A VEGETABLE FARM WITH NO DRUGS FOR THE REST OF YOUR LIVES. DUE TO YOUR PAST RECORDS, YOU MAY STAY TOGETHER. TAKE THEM AWAY."

The room became silent again, all except for the footsteps of Eric and Sheila as they were led away from the great hall to a waiting unit.

"Where to now, Eric? I'm afraid," Sheila offered as she clung to his arm.

"I guess you could say to the conscious world's HELL," replied Eric, although he wasn't too sure as to what lay ahead.

CHAPTER X

Enroute to their confinement, Eric said to Sheila, "I know now why I was chosen for this task. My background with Hitler, my conversion to truth, my knowledge of the power of thought. All these can be used to help these people who are baby-sat by computers . . . their lives lived for them without benefit of thought. My impression now, for our mission, is failure, but we will continue and see what happens. I can recall back in March of the year we were there, the people of Earth were accepting drugs, their music was hypnotic, their combination of corporations and computers becoming overpowering, and finally, the Atomic Power Commission. I can't help wondering if this is what Earth is heading for."

The unit stopped. Eric and Sheila stepped off into a waiting room much like the train stations of old. They witnessed an elderly man being supported by two guards while a decree was read to him by the keeper.

"You are now 65 years old. The Great Computer has rewarded your last moments with the drug trip everyone dreams of." With that, the man was given an overdose and carried off to be cremated.

Sheila spoke up, "Surely they do not kill everyone at 65."

"Yes," replied Eric, "the computer controls the population by life and death."

Just then another unit pulled into the station and a young boy in his teens, along with his younger sister, got off. Eric sensed that both seemed to have some responsive faculties.

The guard accompanying them told the keeper, "Their parents turned them in for incest; as you know the computer rewards parents with an increase in their drug ration for all violations reported."

Hearing that, the young girl began to cry and sobbed, "I did nothing."

Eric knew the girl was telling the truth. The parents more than likely wanted their drug supply increased for they had become saturated to the point of needing further drugs.

Almost immediately, another unit arrived. Only this time several eunuch guards were dragging another eunuch which had drank a portion of concentrated hallucinogens by mistake. The Computer had ruled him contaminated for the possibility of flashbacks happening to him was practically assured, so he was given a life sentence on the farm.

Soon after the guards left, Eric utilized the time to see if he could reach any of the three now in the room. As if by talking to them, he met their minds one at a time. The guard was completely susceptible to Eric's suggestions and so was the young girl. But the boy would not respond. Eric knew that the boy and girl would soon go through withdrawals . . . to the point of death. So taking the girl aside, Eric mentally assured her she would be uncomfortable but would survive. However, he feared for the boy, as he was two years older and had more exposure to the drugs, making his withdrawal more severe.

Just then, a man in his 50's appeared in a door and motioned to them to follow. It was beginning to darken as they left the building, yet Eric could make out mountains all around, implying they were in a valley or dale.

The man spoke, "My name is Jack. I am called the 'Keeper'. As it is not permitted for men and women to sleep together on their first night, the girls will sleep over there." And he pointed to a shack off to one side. "I will call you at 6:00 AM for orientation and breakfast."

Eric, by probing Jack's mind while he talked, assured himself that Jack also was susceptible to thought. He also learned that the camp contained only a few healthy prisoners over the age of forty . . . the rest being sick or dying from lack of drugs.

The next morning, at breakfast, the explanation of what was expected of them was related by the keeper, and the fact that their food would contain no drugs — as punishment. "Anyone not able to work after three days withdrawal, or any slow up in the work, will be cause for extermination. Every three months production that is above quota will be rewarded by everyone having two days off. Working hours are from seven in the morning to five in the evening with other outside duties assigned." With this the keeper turned to leave, adding, "On the whistle, fall out for work in the fields."

The whistle blew and Eric and Sheila joined the others outside in the sunlight, able at last to breathe in clean, fresh air. They picked up their hoes and proceeded to the fields, followed by the eunuch, the young girl, her brother who was now showing signs of extreme nervousness, and a multitude of other Spectrans who Eric knew would not last much longer.

As each continued to work, Eric began to mentally reach the eunuch through thought transference until he was satisfied the eunuch would respond to his thoughts. Eric told him that he was to take the main guard's place in the morning, thereby giving Eric a chance to work on the guard now there. This would leave the camp completely in the hands of Eric, as even the keeper, Jack, would respond to Eric's implanted thoughts.

That evening, Eric and Sheila took up residence and began modest housekeeping. Eric mentioned, "One thing in our favor is that the computers do not control the interior of the camp — only the perimeter."

Just as they were about to relax, the eunuch appeared with the young girl. She had begun to feel the effects of the withdrawal.

"What of her brother?" Eric asked.

"He's dead," replied the eunuch.

Eric gave the young girl the suggestion of being numb to the withdrawal pains and she began to sleep.

Sheila and Eric laid back, propped on elbows, watching the girl.

Sheila said, "What a day! I wonder what the crew of the U-237 would say about this!"

Eric replied, "I would enjoy seeing all of them now. Old Brunt would probably say, 'You get me out of one damn situation and right back in another.'"

Sheila pondered, "The Voice of the Second Dimension didn't miss anything when he described this planet."

"Yes, I agree," replied Eric, "but the only way to save these people was to become one of them. To have done it spiritually, would have made them feel they were on just another of their trips."

Turning away from the girl, Sheila reached over and kissed Eric. "Well, let's hope we can save this planet from this madness. Goodnight, dear."

The next morning, Eric mentally suggested to the eunuch to take his place as guard, for the first guard was given the suggestion to stay by Eric's side. The eunuch responded. Eric then mentally contacted Jack and suggested he bring a water cooler with a wine-colored water jug filled with diluted cocaine.

It was Eric's plan that, from this jug, no more than three cups would be allowed each day to the new arrivals at the farm for the first month; two cups the second month; and then one cup the third month; after that – none. The crematorium would be fired to dispose of those who died.

During the evening, three men in their early twenties were brought to the farm. One was so high he didn't even know his name. Eric knew death was inevitable for him. The other two would die also unless the water worked, and it probably would for the girl now called Beth was drinking the water and holding her own.

On the third day, two of the men entered complete withdrawals while the third, as expected, died from the overdose. Eric gave the other two as much of the diluted drugs as he dared but by the morning of the fourth day, they too were dead. Once more the furnace was fired. Eric now realized that unless he could get to the women that bore the eunuchs, planet Spectra was doomed . . . as even Beth would bear addicted children.

He spent the next few months teaching those of clear mind what the problem was . . . that drugged minds could never see the light of the spirit world. However, it became more apparent that his words were falling on deaf ears. Eric thought to himself, "It's time for drastic action." Then to the group he said aloud, "Watch me! I will lift off the ground and become transparent . . . Watch!" As Eric became transparent and began to rise above the group, they began to sigh and cringe in fear until it dawned on them that Eric was trying to make them understand about the Spirit. Some even began to cry as Eric became visible and returned. "All of this you can do in the spirit world. You only have to listen to what I am telling you." Eric found that he now had the group's attention.

It was learned through these discussions that the women who bred these eunuchs were protected by perfectly-built computerized robots that never talked nor rested and that anyone coming within the posted 'DANGER LIMITS' were killed. From this Eric devised a plan whereas the eunuch guards would play a principal role.

Later, Sheila, in one of her many conversations with Eric, asked, "How can you get around the robots? I know you do not wish to destroy them."

"No, I do not plan to destroy the robots, that is, at least not right away. My thoughts at this point are mixed. I know some of the population will be destroyed in trying to bring this planet to its senses and the robots will be needed to protect what is left after the planet realizes it is doing an about-face. The eunuch breeding camps must be protected, as they are the only clear guarantee I have for the continuation of this planet."

"I can see how they will be useful to us, Eric. It's

just beyond my comprehension as to how we can get control of them."

"Yes, I know, Sheila. I'm going to the mountains to think this whole thing out. I'll be back later."

Eric's mind was filled with thoughts of the Nazi super-race on Earth and the way of life on this planet. He knew they were wrong yet in both cases, he had no choice. The parallel of Spectra's misery to the one now on Earth, was haunting to Eric. He knew drugs had to be completely removed . . . all plants and seeds destroyed . . . nothing must remain . . . not even enough for killing pain was to be left – for it would not be needed. The new offspring would be taught the power of the mind to numb any pain. What was sad to Eric was he knew the present society of addicts were doomed – to be gathered in a field and burned like weeds.

Eric said aloud, "If only the leaders of Earth could visit this place for just one hour to see where they are headed. Truth and trust in God would be most dear to them." With that, Eric, still deep in thought, began his walk back to camp.

CHAPTER XI

Back in camp, Eric found Sheila holding a young girl no more than five years old who had been brought to the farm during his absence. She had accidently taken her parents' drugs.

Sheila implored, "Please, Eric . . . help her. She's in pain."

Eric placed the girl on the ground. "What is your name?"

"Debbie," came the feeble reply.

"Okay, Debbie, we are going to play a game. First, I want you to close your eyes and keep them closed. That's right, now as I begin to count, your eyes will become heavy. So heavy that you won't be able to open them. Now Debbie, while I count backwards, you will get more and more relaxed and want to sleep, a deep sleep, a peaceful sleep. When I reach five, we will be at the age you are now, then as I count lower to four, you will forget everything except your name and what you know about the alphabet and how high you can count. Okay? Here we go . . . 10-9-8-7-6-5-4. Now Debbie, you are four years old. You will remember only what I have told you. You are now three. Again, remember only what I have told you. Now two . . . now one . . . Debbie you are now only one day old and your body requires drugs, but this your mind does not want. You will never have a desire for drugs again. You are now 6 months old; you have learned to crawl but still you have no desire for drugs. You are now two years old, you have been told right from wrong . . . still no desire for drugs. You are now three . . . walking, running, talking, still no desire for drugs. You are now four, Debbie, learning your ABCs and how to count . . . still no desire for drugs. Anytime you wish to control your body say, 'ALPHA'. You will be in a trance state; any cuts or wounds that happen will be healed by placing your hand over it and saying, 'ZETA'. The same with your teeth, when they are healed, say 'OMEGA'.

"Now Debbie, you are five years old and your Aunt Sheila is caring for you. Remember, when I awaken you you will feel a little sick as if you ate something bad, but you will be fine in an hour. Also you will never have a desire for drugs again. You are to obey Sheila as your aunt and you will remember that your parents died when you were born and, above all, Debbie, you are to give respect to all people.

"Okay, Debbie, your head is clear. You are rested. On my count of five, you will awaken . . . 1-2-3-4-5. Awaken!"

Debbie awoke, looked at Sheila and cried, "Aunt Sheila, I don't feel good." With that, Sheila put her arms around her and cried aloud.

Eric thought. "This may be one of the answers to the planet's problem. The next few hours will tell if the suggestion held. If only I could re-program the computers."

Two hours later, Debbie was up and feeling fine. She began to help Sheila, acting as normal as any five year old girl. Eric walked up to her with a vial of drugs but Debbie completely ignored him and the drugs.

"Aunt Sheila," Debbie said, "I'm hungry."

Eric beamed happily for he knew now how to save the planet. As he turned and proceeded into the next room, he came face to face with Johan.

"Johan! How did you get here?" Eric exclaimed, as he grabbed him. "Sheila! Come here, quick!" Eric realized that only he and Sheila could see Johan for he was still in spirit form, not yet assuming Spectran being.

Johan said, "The Voice from the Second Dimension placed me here after my twenty-eight years in the capsule. When I was aboard the sub my last thoughts were to be with you. So here I am. What's going on here?"

Eric brought him up to date and further told him of his plans.

Johan said thoughtfully, "The last radio reports I heard from Earth were of the war trials over our leaders' cremation of people; here you have machines doing the same thing?"

"Yes," Eric replied, "but I now have the means to change all this — by changing the computers . . . YOU!"

"Me?" queried Johan. Then paused in thought. "Yes, I see where I must do it. But how? What plan do you have?"

"First, you must get to the computers and erase all reference to drugs and make it against the law to even own the seed. All traces of drugs must be burned."

"Will not some of the people withdraw and die?" asked Johan.

"Yes . . . some. But we will substitute Kenaf, which looks like marijuana and has no drug effect to it. This will keep their psyche active. Besides, it's the brain food I was looking for . . . very high in protein."

"Next, the machines are to provide only data to the people, not make decisions. Leave them programmed to run the mechanics. No more trials by computer. We will place some of the older men in charge."

Johan asked, "Will they rule justly?"

"Why not?" Eric said, "They have lived with truth so let them apply it. However, Johan, the main point to feed into the computers is that no one under the age of seven is to be sterilized for the next seven years . . . then from that point on — no one."

"You mean all over seven are to be sterilized now?" Johan said disbelievingly.

"Yes, those over seven contain seed that are contaminated. We are going to erase all drug desire from the new young minds, so that by the time they reproduce, the drug effect should be gone."

"Next, Johan, you are to program into the computer an unconscious teaching — by suggestion through television — that from this point on no desire for drugs will be felt and the substitution of mind control along with a moral way of living, will be experienced. We will also suggest no more than two offspring to any one family and allow for self-control."

Sheila asked, "What about the robots?"

"We will leave them around the camps for ten years, then program them for destruction. However, the robots around the computers will remain to prevent any tampering."

"I believe it will work," Johan said excitingly, "but on some of the older addicts, it will be a disaster."

"I know," Eric replied, "but for the overall end it is necessary. But to ease the withdrawals for the younger ones, when they reach the age of seven they will be given three months in the fields on a rotation basis, which should help them to realize the responsibility of survival. We will refer to them as summer camps."

Johan said, "I have had my trip to Earth and saw they have no family togetherness anymore . . . just community living. Drugs are everywhere and the young have no idea of a future, not even a desire. Almost like here. I can see what has to be done. I will go now." And with that, Johan disappeared to re-program the computers.

The next few months began to show the brutal transition of Spectra. The withdrawals and deaths paralleled the Black Death of England in the early years of the planet Earth, with the exception that here, the children remaining when both parents died were fully cared for by the computers. The one thing that Eric had overlooked was the very young did not possess conscious thinking ability.

"I will put them at peace." Johan said . . . and programmed the computers for teaching and the young were mentally satisfied. "I'm glad we won't have any newborns for seven years."

Sheila, meanwhile, had her hands full teaching thought transference to the young. As each age group was reached, Sheila proceeded to the next . . . and the next . . . and the next.

On June 19, 1974, Earth time, all the young finally reached the point of no desire for drugs and were able to control their bleeding, heal themselves, and had learned the moral teachings of the commandments.

Eric then summoned the remaining people to receive the healing process. Meanwhile, Johan began his rounds to the outlying areas, training one man to speak for him. Eventually, these men became leaders in their respective communities.

The following day, while Sheila was telling Debbie a story, and while in a relaxed position, she thought of her early life on Earth at the time her parents were located in the Philippines and wished she was there. This one moment Sheila forgot . . . and disappeared!

CHAPTER XII

Sheila materialized on a beach in the Philippines. When she realized what had happened, the mistake she had made, she began to cry. It was this scene that a roving police unit found and which prompted them to ask 'what happened'. When Sheila would not tell them exactly what was wrong, they took her to the hospital. Sheila, her depression overwhelming, realized she had inherited Earth again and cried aloud, "Eric . . . please."

When Eric returned to camp, Debbie ran to him, crying, "Aunt Sheila . . . she disappeared."

"What!" exclaimed Eric.

"She was telling me a story of her parents on a beach and she disappeared," said Debbie.

"Oh no!" cried Eric, "she's back on Earth!"

Just then Johan appeared. "I know what has happened Eric, is there anything I can do?"

"Who is he?" Debbie asked perplexed.

Eric looked at Debbie in astonishment. "You see Johan?"

Johan replied before Debbie could answer. "Yes, she can see me. I requested the Voice to allow me to remain here for 300 years when I found out how badly I was needed. I took on Spectran form. I know you wish to go to Sheila. I will stay and advise."

"No! Not until I'm sure. I wish to see this test given to me by the Voice of the Second Dimension through to the end. Debbie, Johan will stay with you while I am gone." With that, Eric left for the mountains.

At the top, Eric relaxed completely and asked the Voice to speak to him, but there was only silence. After a few hours passed, Eric cried aloud, "Voice! Speak to me!" Again, there was only silence. Finally, Eric willed himself to the capsule where he confronted the Voice.

"I know why you are here. I know what you desire but it cannot be."

Eric implored, "Johan has elected to stay. I have done my part. Why can't I go?"

"Eric von Wilhelm, we of the 2nd Dimension are satisfied with your work. Yet, you must remain one more year. At that time your wishes will be granted for an eternity. Now return to your work."

Eric immediately reappeared back on the mountain. He thought, 'One year . . . it is a long time, but it will be worth it.' He returned to the city to continue working with Johan and the young people of Spectra. He related to Johan his discussion with the Voice and concluded with, "It's only a little while and we have a lot of work to do."

"Yes, I know," agreed Johan.

Eric began to apply himself day and night. His intake of Kenaf was substantial which kept him going. As time ticked by, Johan and Eric became completely satisfied with the response from the people of Spectra. They knew the people could make it on their own now.

On the evening of December 12, 1974, Earth time, Johan came to Eric. "It is time to go to the mountain."

"What do you mean?" queried Eric.

"You'll see," replied Johan, "in the morning, you'll see."

The next morning both men transited the mountain. Upon arriving Johan spoke. "Eric, I have requested another 300 years here which means that I am now obligated to stay on Spectra for 600 years. You are free to go now, if you wish."

The Voice spoke to both men. "From this date forward, you, Johan, will be known as 'Metha of Spectra'. You Eric von Wilhelm have earned a status equal to mine . . . the Universe is yours. Eric von Wilhelm will now be known as the 'Voice of the Second Galactic Dimension'. I say to you Metha, that your sacrifice will be rewarded upon your death in 600 years." A silence followed, then the Voice continued.

"For you Eric von Wilhelm, we will give Earth a display today to announce your arrival. Remember to use the pyramids in your transition."

Eric turned to Metha and said, "You only have to call me and I will be here."

"I know. Now go, Sheila is in much need of you."

Eric began his transition to Earth on December 13th, 1974. A great eclipse was in progress as Eric arrived in the Southwestern part of the United States via an old pyramid. Having taken his original form, Eric immediately began to formulate plans to get to Sheila.

By now, most of the men that were on the U-237 were nearing their sixties, well-settled, and had most of their families raised.

Captain Brunt and Melvin Schmidt were aboard their ship in the Gulf of Mexico when they felt the call from Eric to proceed to a Mexican port. When Eric came aboard he explained briefly of the past years, and then with full fuel aboard, they set sail for the South Pacific.

Once underway, Eric further explained to Captain Brunt and Schmidt about his experiences and stated that in the near future they would have to choose between this way of life and that which Eric promised.

Coinciding with Eric's arrival, Sheila began to receive his thoughts and began to ready herself to leave the hospital and meet them at the port. Her spirits were high and she was so excited when she told the nurse that she would be leaving soon, forever, that the nurse figured she must have really lost all control of her mind. However, it was the nurse who almost lost her mind the following day when it was discovered that Sheila was missing from her room and the grounds.

Sheila materialized at the port of Cebu Harbor in the Philippines and her thought waves began getting stronger as the upcoming meeting with Eric approached.

The evening of January 12th, 1975, saw a small

ship pull into port. Sheila ran to the edge of the dock. On board, she could see Captain Brunt and Schmidt, but not Eric. They tied up and upon seeing Sheila, Brunt and Schmidt realized that the story Eric had told them was true. After hugging them both, Sheila asked, "Where is Eric?"

"Behind you," replied Eric, immediately holding Sheila close as she embraced him and began kissing him repeatedly. "There, there, Sheila, we will have an eternity for this."

Eric stepped away from Sheila and walked to the dock. Sheila followed closely, afraid of losing him again. Eric emitted a mental suggestion that no one present near or at the dock would remember their presence. Then they boarded the ship and started below.

"Where to, Eric?" questioned Brunt.

Eric replied, "Port Everglades, Florida."

EPILOG

As the bow of the ship cut through the water, Eric stood on the deck transmitting his thoughts to the crew of the U-237 located in various places in the United States.

The remaining crewmen began to receive his thoughts. They were to meet him in Port Everglades on February 12th, 1975. They being: Carl Schultz—now 50; Oscar Hiney—70; Verne Hagen—51; Paul Rumal—53; Peter Loften—52; Paul Durbin—53; Herman Kofcher—54; Heinrich Goulstadt—54 and Carl Hinze—now only 42 due to his half-life. They were to tell all who asked that they were going on a deep sea fishing trip and holiday.

The day of February 12th saw a group of men assembled at the dock as the ship pulled into port. Once the ship was berthed and each man came aboard, he immediately was allowed to review his past life in America — knowing it as a dream and recalling once again their life aboard the submarine. All assembled aboard, Eric stepped to the dock to erase any awareness of their presence. However, as the ship docked, one young lad remembering the story of its disappearance, had taken off to tell the authorities. Eric mentally realized the situation and returned quickly to the ship. "Willie! We must set out to sea! At once!"

"Where to?" Captain Brunt asked.

Eric replied, "28° North, 77.5° West."

Then began the re-telling of Eric's story covering the past thirty years for his fellow crewmen.

"How are we to know this is true?" queried Carl Hinze.

"All of you remember when Sheila disappeared. Well she is here among you now. What more proof do you need?"

Sheila spoke up. "I have been there and I long to

be there again. Even I must go through this transition again."

"But we will all die," spoke Sam Jones.

"Yes, by Earth standards. But you will feel no discomfort. Now come, our time is short. All those wishing to join me will jump overboard and swim to the sub, for I have chosen the U-237 as my means of conveyance to the other dimension."

Without hesitation Sheila went forward and jumped into the water and began diving towards the sub. Captain Brunt and Melvin Schmidt were next to follow, then the remaining crew until only Sam Jones and Eric remained aboard.

"I can't do it! I wish to remain here on Earth." implored Sam Jones. "There is so much I can do here."

"Very well then, you will remain." At that moment the U-237 surfaced alongside the ship. As Eric stepped to the sub and it began to disappear, Eric told Carl, "Use your time wisely, my friend."

As the Coast Guard towed the missing ship back to port, below deck, the ship's doctor was trying to make sense from Sam Jones' story. The doubt was beginning to show in his face. "Again," the doctor thought, "another strange and mysterious tale of the Devil's Triangle which has taken its toll . . ."

BUT IS IT THE **DEVIL'S** TRIANGLE?

FORTHCOMING NEPTUNE BOOKS

STARRING JOHN WAYNE
CASSANDRA–A PILLAR OF SALT
ANNIE LAURIE (OF THE RIVER AIRE)
DOS COMPADRES
AMERICA'S CENTENNIAL CELEBRATION
(Philadelphia–1876)
THE SUN NEVER SHINES